The Future of Local Economic Development

This book looks at the future role of local economic development. Once New Labour came to power in 1997, they sought a third way between the new right agenda of Thatcherism with its attempts to reduce the role of the local state and foster a free market and the left's attempts to take more control over the local economy in the interest of workers. In July 2007, Gordon Brown's government published the 'Review of Sub-national Economic Development and Regeneration'.

This book argues that competitiveness and neo-liberalism, or increased market domination over an ever wider range of social relations, have in reality dominated New Labour's policies. Yet a number of contradictions remain as New Labour continues to seek a reduction in poverty and regional and local disparities. The book analyses the changes that will result from further market domination under the Sub-national Review but also the opportunities that will arise for local economic development agents, particularly those with a concern for social justice. It looks specifically at regional and sub-regional strategy making; partnership, networking and building institutional capacity; local labour market policy and policy towards cities. An additional feature of the book is that several authors draw on international comparisons.

This book was published as a special issue of *Local Economy*.

Ines Newman is Principal Research Fellow at the Warwick Business School, United Kingdom.

The Future of Local Economic Development

Edited by Ines Newman

Routledge
Taylor & Francis Group
LONDON AND NEW YORK

First published 2010 by Routledge
2 Park Square, Milton Park, Abingdon, Oxon, OX14 4RN

Simultaneously published in the USA and Canada
by Routledge
270 Madison Avenue, New York, NY 10016

Routledge is an imprint of the Taylor & Francis Group, an informa business

Typeset in Helvetica by Value Chain, India
Printed and bound in Great Britain by TJI Digital, Padstow, Cornwall

British Library Cataloguing in Publication Data
A catalogue record for this book is available from the British Library

ISBN10: 0-415-55126-9
ISBN13: 978-0-415-55126-7

Contents

Preface: Local Economic Development in the Credit Crunch

This set of articles on the future of local economic development was written before the 'credit crunch' or crisis in the financial sector. Yet the significant downturn in the economy has reinforced, rather than undermined, the arguments put forward around the contradictions in current government policy and the scope and importance of local economic development.

In my introduction, written in early 2008, I drew on the work of Matthew Watson in arguing that Gordon Brown was pursuing what might be termed a 'neo Adam Smith' agenda in his asset based welfare model underpinned by the belief in self disciplining financial agents pursuing their own interest. Brown fostered what Nunn and Johnson have called 'flexicurity' or an attempt to create employment opportunities through competitiveness rather than job security. This insecurity has been made acceptable through a high return for those that invested in assets: their home, financial assets or the stock exchange. The Department of Trade and Industry disappeared to be replaced by the Department of Business, Enterprise and Regulatory Reform designed to support finance, risk and less regulation.

The contributors to this publication emphasized the contradictions in this approach, contradictions that are made more evident by its collapse. The high returns to assets increase inequalities: spatially as money is invested where returns to assets are highest and individually as there are no compensation for those without assets and in poor quality employment with cyclical returns to dependence on benefits. The policy ties investment into increasing land values and other speculative activities rather than raising productive activity. It sharpens the environmental problems as it fails to deal with limited resources and prioritises competitiveness over sustainability.

At national level the focus has so far been on underwriting and propping up what Colin Crouch has called 'privatised Keynesism'[1]. Keynes advocated

---

[1]A full explanation can be heard on the podcast of a paper '*The role of financial risk in privatized Keynesism*' given in September 2008 at a University of Warwick workshop on The Political Economy of the Subprime Crisis http://www2.warwick.ac.uk/newsandevents/audio/more/spc/?podcastItem=subprime3a.mp3

the state raising debt and financing public works to encourage consumption in a recession while, over the last thirty years, the focus has switched to raising private debt to fuel the economy. Crouch argues that the bail out of the banks and the attempts to stimulate private consumption will further support the growth of private debt because consumers and speculators will now believe that irresponsible behaviour will be underwritten by the State. This may fuel the threat to cities (see Turok's contribution) posed by an inflated, debt fuelled consumer spending boom that leads to speculative building rather than investment in infrastructure and the quality of life. However Crouch suggests we will also see the rise of a more corporatist state as bankruptcies, mergers and acquisitions combined with State funding and the continuing contradiction of inequality push the focus onto corporate social responsibility. The increased focus on corporate social responsibility could provide some opportunities.

In our original article in 1999, which was the starting point for this book, Mike Geddes and I suggested another scenario or set of starting points or principles. In this scenario lessons are learnt from challenges to the market model in the South and the European 'social model' and a greater focus is placed on addressing environmental threats and on elevating the principles of social justice over those of competitiveness. The contributors here show that this remains a major challenge. But they also indicate possibilities for local economic development agents to pursue a more radical agenda. The return of Keynesianism risks preoccupation with macro policy and finance to the exclusion of local and regional differences in the real economy. The local economic development agent must ensure that there is a strong local dimension to economic policy and that the opportunities offered by the world of corporate social responsibility are developed locally and regionally to address local needs. The task of pursuing an alternative scenario at local level has become even more urgent.

Ines Newman
Editor

VIEWPOINT

Regions, Economies and Planning in England after the Sub-national Review

TIM MARSHALL

Enter the SNR

The review of sub-national economic development and regeneration aimed to take a fresh look at how central government coordinated its input to the economy below the national level, specifically with the regional agencies it had created in 1999 and with local authorities. From the start of the Blair government the deep split in Labour ranks over the regional issue, covering up even deeper splits on the approach to neoliberal economic policy, meant that even the moderate and quite economically biased approach of the Millan (Regional Policy Commission, 1996) report was not quite implemented. Millan had recommended that the RDAs should be set up by regional chambers, and be responsible to them. The switch to control to a business-led board, responsible to the secretary of state, was a critical one, changing the drive and sense of the regionalist project at its start. This was then followed by the defeat of any return to the fuller regionalist programme represented by the voting down of an elected assembly for the North East in 2004.

What came out of this review, in the published report of July 2007 (HM Treasury *et al.* 2007)? Different observers have taken different perspectives. Many local councils welcomed what they saw as a commitment to passing more economic responsibility to locally led agencies, away from RDAs, linked into the evolving LAA and emerging MAA regimes. RDAs were also clearly encouraged by being given the lead role on a single regional strategy, following the abolition of the regional assemblies in 2010. The regional assemblies made remarkably little noise at their abolition, a matter which warrants some reflection. Overall the package was met without excitement but without any major opposition from key interests.[1]

Key Features of the 1998–2008 Regional Regime

It is worth reminding ourselves again what this system has been since the RDAs began. This has been by no means 'indicative planning' in the sense discussed and sometimes practised in the 1960s and 1970s (in France for example). 'Plan' is not part of New Labour language, which has managed to exclude the word from all the regionally related legislation since 1997 (though it is interesting that we are to be given the Infrastructure Planning Commission, possibly indicating the word is acceptable in safe hands). RDAs have prepared 'strategies', as has every other regional actor; 'frameworks' is the other preferred term. The difference is not purely linguistic, but indicates a lower ambition to direct, more akin to business practice, where risk and uncertainty is the norm. The most seriously prepared of these strategies have doubtless been the RSSs of the last four years, but they lack implementation commitment from government, which has its headline interest (housing numbers) and little else. Regional Economic Strategies on the other hand have been lighter, promotional documents, but have had real financial backing. It is no doubt partly this messy and unsatisfying multiple asymmetry in the regime which meant that many weary operators hardly thought it worthy of passionate defence against the SNR.

The RDAs have not been independently reviewed over their ten year lifespan, so it is impossible to say whether they have in any sense deserved the victory over the assemblies which the sub-national review marks. (I am aware of the numerous evaluative exercises, from those by the RDAs themselves, to those by ministries and select committees; but none of these are fully independent of government; Pearce, 2008, summarises the position well). Have they made a real difference to economic success, however defined? We may guess that with the resources spent, some difference has indeed been made, but the evidence, as far as I am aware, is not to hand. Until a full and genuinely independent review is available, an agnostic position might be the most appropriate one for commentators. So moving on to something new is necessarily a leap in the dark.

An Extraordinary Institutional Shift?

How far has government managed to make a 'new sense' of the landscape, and how significant will the detailing be as it emerges during 2008?

This is where the largest disagreements of interpretation are likely. My view is that this is a major and very extraordinary reorientation of state policy. Unless local authorities are given something cast iron like a 'dual key' control over the content of the draft single regional strategy, then it is clear that regional planning and strategising has been passed to a very new sort of body. This body, the RDA, is state sponsored, funded and legitimised, and managed on behalf of government by a business led board. For example, the current board for the South East RDA, SEEDA, has eight business people, one of whom chairs it, as well as four elected councillors, one trade unionist and a university vice chancellor. It is hardly surprising that this board has taken a consistently bullish approach to regional growth, in spite of the widespread consensus in the wider south east society that the region is 'bursting at the seams', as many pundits would phrase it. Because the RDA is now to prepare a strategy which combines the strategies for economic development, physical planning, housing and transport, it will in principle be more influential than the strategising processes of 1990–2010, when a wide range of diverse strategies were prepared by diverse agencies – even though normally with the critical final versions set by one government ministry or another.

The extraordinariness of this government decision therefore needs emphasis. A body set up to be subservient to 'regional society', in the shape of a regional chamber (in the Millan original schema), is instead to be the dominant figure in the regional landscape, not just for economic issues but across the board. Of course how the new regional architecture is actually set up will be critical, and I come back to this later. But a clearer step towards 'de-democratisation' or 'post democracy', as increasingly prevalent features of the neoliberal state, would be hard to imagine.

Arguing Through What the Changes Represent

But weren't all these strategising public processes characterised by partnership and limited public involvement, with the final decision always resting with central government? And won't the new regime, which will emerge during 2008, be essentially the same, with a grand coalition of regional elites and central government, just making the real power relations much clearer than in the past? Nothing essential will change.

I disagree with this argument, though admit some truth in it. Yes it will remain a governance network, but there are governance networks and governance networks, as work by Skelcher and colleagues has very well clarified in recent research (Klijn & Skelcher, 2007, for example) – their 'democraticness' depends on very particular design and behaviour. Two essential differences will very likely arise from the new regional governance system. The main one is of power. Any priorities that do not coincide with those of the government of the day will fail to find a place in the new strategising and decision-making processes. Oppositional interests will have even less hand holds. Certainly the regional assembly system, and local authority-led regime of the 1990s were very imperfect machineries, but access was available to legitimate actors in most pressure groups and in elected local governments. Will such potentially influential access be available under the new arrangements?

The second reason is that the changes embed new language. The language of the RDAs is that of business and the competitiveness agenda, of managerialism and the rhetoric of markets. The discourses of the assemblies have been significantly different, reflecting much more varied sources, environmental, social, public. It is certainly the case that central government discourse is strongly influenced by economistic phrasing, spreading through planning documents and practice, as in other spheres of public policy (education, health and so on). But up to the present the regional public policy assemblage has contained diverse formulas. The probability in the new system is that this mixed discourse and the thinking it carries and maintains will be reduced in complexity and richness.

Potential Positive Aspects of the Changes

Given the negative judgement here on most of the current policy direction, it is important to note some aspects which have at least some potential for improving the operation of planning and governing in the regions. One is that for integration. This linking, for example to Agencies and central programmes (in say transport or energy) has always been an Achilles heel of regional planning, and if the greater and more coherent clout of the RDAs can give better results in this way, this may be worthwhile. Much may depend on the role of the Government Offices for the Regions, which will need to work much more as a two way conduit, not just funnelling down central priorities. Another key link will be to the Infrastructure Planning Commission, which will further weaken regional and local voices (unless redesigned in a way to avoid that result).

Another potentially interesting constitutional step was the appointment of 'regional ministers' and giving a select committee a role in relation to regions under the Governance of Britain initiative. However these remain uncertain in their impact, and are as likely to fade away quietly as to start to rebalance central–regional relations.

One other hope is that the research and data base can be further improved, given greater resources and well targeted programmes.

Table 1. Content of suggested strategies under new system

Scale of strategising	Nature of strategies
Regional	'Single' strategy (probably including spatial planning, housing, environment and economy), slimline content specifying key quantitative directions and timescales, but without sub-regional or local detail. Implementation plans as required for key matters to be progressed at regional level, to deal with 3–5 year period.
Sub-regional	Most likely several strategies, covering main sectoral needs (spatial planning, economy, environment), both for long-term guidance and for implementation. Whether of this form or 'single', some at least (spatial planning, economic) would be formally part of the SRS, and all have to conform with it.
Local	LDFs, SCSs, plus other sectoral strategies as needed (economic, regeneration etc).

Regional assemblies have done much to improve understandings of what is going on in their regions, and regional observatories, jointly run with RDAs, may be able to become genuinely cross-sectoral monitoring and analysing organisations, as against often being run on a shoestring and rather sidelined from questions of power. Working alongside the National Housing and Planning Advice Unit could facilitate genuinely independent and regionally sensitive debates on evidence – what counts, what doesn't.

Rebalancing the New System

Some will see this interpretation as jaundiced and pessimistic. Surely the RDAs will change their character of necessity when their brief is widened beyond economy? What might a more positive prospect look like, from my viewpoint? The central government working group developing the details of the new system between July 2007 and February 2008 had two main challenges. One was to establish what a single regional strategy might look like, the other was to decide what sort of guidance to give to regions on the processes for agreeing a (draft) single regional strategy. I will just make some suggestions on these here (some summary points are given in Tables 1 and 2).

Content of the Single Regional Strategy

The first depends on how far the whole strategy is to be statutory, and on the degree of detail that should be incorporated into it, across strategic areas (economic, spatial, housing etc) and across levels (all regional,

Table 2. Arrangements for making strategies suggested for new system

Scale of strategising	Arrangements for preparing strategies
All levels	Cross expertise working groups should be brought into strategy formation (local government, pressure groups, agencies), and far wider public communication and involvement approaches should be pursued, above all at the key single strategy regional level.
Regional	'Single' strategy to be prepared by RDA and local government and other partners, with joint sign off of strategy by RDA board and local government parliament, before central government takes over decision making. Implementation plans also to be jointly prepared and agreed.
Sub-regional	Strategies to be prepared by local government bodies in subregion, in conformity with SRS.
Local	LDFs and SCSs prepared by local government bodies, in conformity with SRS and sub-regional strategies.

sub-regional, even local). A first point to make is that it is absolutely unlikely that the strategy will really be single. The new strategic landscape will be leaner and cleaner, but is bound to contain strategies that cannot be contained in a tolerably concise document – regeneration, culture, health, skills, environmental sectors, waste – these are just a few fields which may still justifiably be separately strategised on at the regional scale. Nevertheless as far as the 'single' strategy is concerned, I would argue for leaving as much as possible to lower tiers of government, given that these will have the democratic legitimacy which the RDA lacks. However, it is clear that following the abolition of structure plans, there is a serious gap between regions and all but the largest authorities (such as some of the new unitary counties like Cornwall). This is one argument for handing planmaking and strategising powers to sub-regional units, be those new large unitaries, or combinations or possibly divisions of unitaries, districts or counties (Table 1).

This is clearly against the grain of government policy, but would have clear advantages for integrated and legitimate governance at sub-regional level, across a wide range of policy areas. The single regional strategy would then oversee a cluster of sub-regional strategies. No doubt the sub-regional strategies, whether single or clustered, would be nested in legislative terms within the regional SRS, and of course would have to conform with it. But within those limits they could be powerful plans, as separable modules within the system, prepared by local government in open and participatory manner, and revised as necessary on appropriate timescales on the decision of those local governments.

Secondly, the single regional strategy would also be shorn of detail, because much of this would be placed in nonstatutory implementation schemes. These would be prepared and implemented in pure partnership mode, even though benefiting largely from RDA funding. By pure partnership is meant genuine agreement of RDA and local government, joint keys as well as joint implementation. The implementation schemes would exist in as large a number as was found to be useful, at a minimum for key areas such as transport, housing, economy and environmental management. A major issue is how far government departments would then commit to implementing such schemes. Implementation and delivery will still be at the heart of the regional question.

Governance of the New Regional System

Finally, what about control of the evolution of the single regional strategy? This should have three key elements. If each region creates a sort of regional parliament to represent to the RDA regional opinions, this body should have a sign off power for the draft single strategy. This would clearly not be the reinvention of assemblies by another name, because such a body would have a much less continuous and more virtual existence with a minimal secretariat, and few regular meetings (medieval parliaments used to meet perhaps every year or two, at most, for a few days – but with clear powers). The voting membership of the regional 'senate' should be a cross section of locally elected councillors, representing fair political and spatial balances in each region.

The second element would be structures of working groups not unlike the systems used to build regional planning guidance, though with far wider membership to concentrate the appropriate wider expertise needed by a single strategy approach (Table 2).

The third key process feature in the making of the single strategy would be a massive improvement to the publicity and involvement processes. Much fuller regional debates should be facilitated, using all media, with much larger budgets than has been available to RSS producers recently. Given the potential power of the Single Regional Strategy (and its implementation programmes), it is essential that public access is an absolute principle. This should be complemented by a truly open and strategic examination in public process, again linked by current media techniques so that every interest and individual has at least the potential to see what future is being decided for each region. In particular, funds should be provided for groups with fewer resources, so that nongovernmental priorities can get equally full hearings.

At the time of writing, these issues are not decided. There may be a chance to take some of the better features of the current system and incorporate some genuinely democratic and integrated facets into what will otherwise look like a depressing shift to an elite and unattractive institutional system. So there is something at stake in the arguments of 2008.

Note

1. It should be noted that this commentary is written before the central government was due to report on how it proposed to progress the sub-national review agenda. Some points may therefore look outdated by the time of publication.

References

HM Treasury, Department for Business, Enterprise and Regulatory Reform, and Communities and Local Government (2007) *Review of Sub-national Economic Development and Regeneration* (London: The Stationery Office).

Klijn, E. & Skelcher, C. (2007) Democracy and governance networks: Compatible or not? *Public Administration*, 85(3), pp. 587–608.

Pearce, G. (2008) Institutional capacity in the English regions, in: J. Bradbury (Ed) *Devolution, Regionalism and Regional Development*, pp. 97–116 (Abingdon: Routledge).

Regional Policy Commission (1996) *Renewing the Regions: Strategies for Regional Economic Development* (Sheffield: Sheffield Hallam University).

VIEWPOINT

The Future of Economic Development after the Sub-national Review

GREG CLARK

There is new deal for economic development in the UK (well in England at least). It involves increased strategic power for a regional tier, larger implementation roles and greater access to local tax base for local government, and an enhanced coordinating role for Government.

As the UK Government roles out its sub-national review of economic development and regeneration we can see more clearly what lies ahead. The introduction of a wider use of economic development companies at the local level to deliver public/private engagement is a welcome sign, and the shift towards better integrated economic, physical, and environmental planning at regional level must surely be a good thing. But what are the bigger signs and changes that this heralds?

Perhaps the first broader observation is that local economic development is now fully part of the main stream apparatus of policy for driving economic performance. This may seem unsurprising to some, but it is only 20 years ago that local economic development in the UK was seen primarily as a vehicle for opposition and alternative approaches to managing the decline of traditional industries. Local economic development policy had 'opposi-tional' over tones then, but is now fully part of the national effort to boost productivity led growth (Table 1).

The next observation is the increasing integration of economic development policies with those of transport, housing, land use, and environment at the regional level. We can discern some important trends here. Firstly, the clear desire from government to ensure that

Table 1. Evolution of Regional Policies 1950s to 2000s in OECD Countries

	Traditional Regional Policies 'Regional Planning' 1950s to 1990s	**New Regional Policies** 'Territorial Development' 1980s to present
Objectives	Balance national economies by compensating for disparities	Increasing regional development performance in all regions.
Strategies	Sectoral approach	Integrated development programmes and projects at regional level.
Geog focus	Political/Administrative Regions	Economic regions
Target	Lagging regions and local economies	All regions and local economies.
Context	National economy	International economy
Tools	Subsidies, incentives, state aids, and regulations	Assets, drivers of growth, soft and hard infrastructures
Actors	National governments	Multiple levels of governments and private/civic actors

Adapted from the OECD.

environmental considerations and imperatives are integrated into the way economic development plans are formulated, overcoming the perception of competing priorities and instead to find means of integrating them. No small task, but essential to attempt. Next we might observe that the integration of housing, planning, transport, and economic development is long overdue. How could any of us have believed that it was possible to substantially influence local economic performance without a consideration of other policies such as planning, transport, and housing? It seems ludicrous now, but of course, this is now.

One benefit of the Treasury's productivity and growth framework is that it reminds us that investment, skills, enterprise, employment, and innovation are all connected together, so we need to plan them together. Of course, New Zealand readers will know that their Growth and Innovation framework has been doing this for a few years now, and colleagues in Canada will remark at the similarities to their Provincial Prosperity agendas.

In addition, we might observe that there is now a new emphasis on the objective for all local economies to succeed. This may come as no surprise overall, but it does mean that the local economic development tool box has to be adaptable to fast growing successful places as well as to those that are still in transition. In this respect the review places the UK at the centre of contemporary thinking about sub-national economic development in a global age.

Lastly, the striking and exciting new dimension in the UK, is the beginning of a process to develop new financial resources, and hence new leadership roles, for local government. Policy change may move slowly, but following the Lyons review we begin to see not simply some innovative, modest local finance tools, but also renewed confidence and vigour amongst local leaders about how to use what tools and assets they already have. It appears that there is a new freedom and will to innovate.

In countries all over the world, but especially in the USA and in some parts of Asia, local fiscal and financial freedoms are the driving force behind local economic development policy. This certainly brings risks, but it also makes local governments substantially responsible for, and responsive to, local economic performance. This helps to make Local Government more entrepreneurial and more innovative, and sometimes more competitive. It means that mistakes can be made, but also that great local leadership can emerge and succeed.

FEATURES

Introduction: The Future of Local Economic Development

INES NEWMAN

In May 1999, Mike Geddes and I published a article in Local Economy, *Evolution and Conflict in Local Economic Development*, in a special issue to commemorate the life of Sam Aaronovitch, the founder of the journal. The article sought to trace and analyse the debate over the direction of government policy looking as we said 'at the conflicts between new right and new left approaches in the 1980s and the 'New Centrism' that has emerged from this struggle in the 1990s'.

We argued in that article that the principles for local economic development that came out of 'new centrism', (the balance between competition and collaboration; the importance of supply conditions, especially training; partnership; a strengthened regional context; and the increasing importance of 'sustainability' and community economic development) all embodied significant tensions and conflicts.

As the 'Blair' period, which was characterised by Antony Giddens' 'Third Way', ends and we move into the 'Brown regime' it is timely to re-examine the issues we raised. Is the Brown agenda, set out in the recent sub-national review (HM Treasury *et al.*, 2007), likely to resolve these tensions and if so what does that mean in terms of who will benefit from future policy direction? Furthermore what does it mean for the role of the economic development officer, particularly those on the left with a concern for social justice?

This article is divided into three sections and serves as an introduction to the other articles in this special issue of *Local Economy*, which look at policy towards cities (Ivan Turok), labour markets (Alex Nunn and Steve Johnson) and new approaches to developing softer outcomes such as building networks, partnerships and institutional capacity (Graham Haughton and Phil Allmendinger), and the *In Perspective* section, which looks at the future role of economic development practitioners from a variety of those currently involved in the field. The first section of this article looks back at ten years of the Labour Party and the 'third way' agenda and the tensions we originally identified and asks what has happened in these. The second section outlines the Brown era and lists the policy changes that are to be anticipated as a result of the sub-national review. The final section of this article identifies where I believe there is still scope for progressive policies within local economic development.

Looking Back Over 10 Years of New Labour

The Dominance of Neoliberalism

In 2004 Antony Giddens sought to justify his influential term 'the third way' by claiming it was just a label to cover all attempts to find a 'revisionist social democracy':

> The Third Way, as I have always understood it, is simply a label for the renewal of social democracy. Centre-left parties across the world have revised their doctrines in the light of social and economic changes: the disappearance of socialist utopias, globalisation, the development of a service economy and ageing populations. In the face of these, the First Way – classical social democracy, based on Keynesianism and traditional statism – has become largely obsolete. The Second Way – Thatcherism or free-market fundamentalism – proved a disastrous alternative. The aim of Third Way thinking – revisionist social democracy – is to create policies for the centre left that respond to these changes. (Giddens, 2004)

Interestingly Brown has only used the term 'the third way' once over the last ten years (Lee, 2006). Its vagueness and failure to provide an intellectual framework for a left-centre approach may be the main cause of his rejection. But more significantly those on the left studying New Labour's record have shown that the last ten years have been dominated by neoliberalism and that, despite the rhetoric, policy development has been very close to Thatcher's free market fundamentalism. Neoliberalism is here taken in the wide sense of a 'framework of disciplinary political authority that enforces market rule over an ever wider range of social relations throughout the world economy' (Brenner & Theodore, 2002, p. 14)

At a recent seminar on Labour and Planning organised by Tim Marshall and Andy Inch (see http://www.pnuk.org.uk/newlabour.htm and forthcoming *Planning Practice and Research*) Stuart Wilks-Heeg (2007) from Liverpool University argued that New Labour had succeeded in successfully implementing failed Conservative neo liberal policies. He gave four examples.

- The 1998 Education Act sought to introduce grant maintained schools and City Technology colleges but only succeeded in creating 15 City Technology Colleges. We now have proposals for 128 city academies by 2009.
- The 1988 Housing Act promoted large scale voluntary transfer of housing estates but by 1992 only 1.9% (15) had transferred contrasted by 2006 when 148 authorities had transferred their stock.
- The 1988 Local Government Act introduced compulsory competitive tendering but 80% of service provision remained in house. Now with the emphasis on choice, contestability, value for money and pressure through the comprehensive performance assessment, privatisation is accelerating.
- The Conservatives introduced the private finance initiative (PFI). The scheme was moderately successful in health and transport but only one local authority signed a PFI scheme under the Conservatives. In total 34 PFI schemes were agreed in the ten years 1986–1996, worth £2 billion. Since New Labour came to power the scheme has been revamped and in the following ten years, 1996–2006, 549 PFI schemes were agreed worth £51 billion including many local authority PFI schemes.

This argument has also been made strongly by Stuart Hall (2007, pp. 119–120):

> New Labour's long-term mission seems to be, broadly, the transformation of social democracy into a particular variant of free-market neo-liberalism. . . . In the first phase of the so-called neo-liberal revolution, Thatcherism installed the enterprise culture and 'market forces' at the heart of society, in the effort to dismantle reformist and redistributive 'welfare' habits and expectations. An economic logic organized around 'the market' became entrenched as the new social discourse, the sole measure of efficiency and social value. New Labour has taken this first phase as its platform, expanding 'marketization' as a general approach not only to the public services, but to the 'modernization' of the public sphere and all the wider institutions of civil society and social governance – spheres traditionally associated with Labour – which have hitherto evaded the full rigours and disciplines of a market logic.

Alan Finlayson (2003) has looked particularly at the use of the term 'modernisation' by New Labour as a conceptual hook to reconcile a neoliberal analysis (putting growth high on the agenda) with social democracy. Modernisation was linked to metaphors of nature – it was something you have to adapt to, you need to 'modernise or die'. But it was also a 'historic opportunity' to be tackled by 'new' Labour. Finlayson points out that there is a fundamental contradiction between these two uses of modernisation – how can modernisation be something you have to live with and at the same time be an active innovative policy? But, despite this contradiction, the terms 'Modernisation' and 'New' have served the government well for, like motherhood and apple pie, you cannot be against modernisation. After ten years, modernisation is now fading as a metaphor but increasingly there is an appeal to hegemony: 'You can't possibly think/believe!' Stuart Hall argues that this hegemony has been achieved by using consumer choice and diversity as levers to prize the state open for creeping privatisation and conceptualising the government, on the Tesco's model, as a 'delivery' system. Delivery becomes the function of government undermining the very notion of a public sphere or a 'public interest' and what remains are apolitical matters of the technicalities of administration, the delivery of services and the 'governance' of society.

Crispian Fuller and Mike Geddes (forthcoming 2008) have drawn on Peck and Tickell's (2002) concept of 'roll-out neo liberalism' with the state seeking to further embed neoliberalism while also trying to address the contradictions and tensions arising from it. Haughton and Allmendinger in their article in this special issue pursue a similar theme when they talk about 'metagovernance' with the nation state reworking and rescaling responsibilities across the tiers of governance and retaining control through its strategic selectivity about who it lends powers to, on what terms and how it chooses to redraw and redefine its distribution of powers over time.

Yet despite the dominance of neoliberalism and marketisation and the broad policy orientations towards privatisation, workfare employment policies and a market bias, the tensions we identified in our article ten years ago have not diminished. New Labour does still hanker over a reduction in child poverty, an end to discrimination and saving the planet from climate change.

Continuing Tensions

Alex Nunn and Steve Johnson in their article in this special issue argue that competitiveness is seen as fundamental but that New Labour has dealt with the tension between competitiveness and collaboration by seeing collaboration and networked governance as a way of delivering competitiveness. This theme is picked up in Graham Haughton and Phil Allmendinger's article in this special issue, which argues that the very process of partnership and collaboration creates its own pressures for conformity, if not unity, in agreeing which behaviours and visions are deemed acceptable to the majority of partners. So it could be argued that there is no longer a tension between competitiveness and collaboration. Collaboration is now used to further competitiveness. This is also being promoted by Multi Area Agreements (MAAs) and by the agenda for shared services and two tier pathfinders which are likely to result in further privatisation.

While this overall trend is both important to observe and certainly underpins how New Labour has tried to address the tensions, some tensions still remain. It is clear that 'place making' as the key function of local government sets a very competitive agenda and is very far away from previous definitions that centred on the welfare role of local government.

However, this does not sit easily with government aims to reduce the differential growth between regions. As Ivan Turok argues in his article in this special issue, there are tensions 'between focusing on core cities as new-found drivers of contemporary growth' rather than older less competitive towns and cities and between encouraging London as a world city and encouraging development in the North. The results is a growing divide between rich and poor with less and less room in the south for those households who are neither rich nor poor who have either moved elsewhere, or become poor (Dorling *et al.*, 2007).

There has been a significant shift in the tensions between flexible labour markets and good quality employment under New Labour with emphasis on work as a way out of poverty linked to improved working rights and conditions: the minimum wage; tax credits; maternity and paternity leave; part time employment rights; reforms to the regulation of the transfer of public employees with pensions and working conditions covered for local authority workers; and the introduction of trade union learning reps. However, half the children in poverty are in a household with an adult in work (Palmer *et al.*, 2007) and work is clearly not always offering a route out of poverty. Furthermore, there is considerable churn at the bottom end of the labour market into and out of employment (job outcomes for mandatory New Deal participants have fallen to 40% for under 25s, and under 30% for over 25s; Simmonds, 2007) with problems of debt exacerbated by the benefits system failing to deliver benefits as soon as someone falls back into worklessness. Alex Nunn and Steve Johnson talk about 'flexicurity' with the attempt to create employment opportunities through competitiveness rather than job security. This focus on employment is underpinned by the focus on cities (see Turok's article in this special issue) and the RDA target of an 80% employment rate and a skills target rather than any target on pay or on reducing unemployment. There is still not enough attention to the aspects of the Freud report that called for long-term support to raise employees out of in-work poverty and poor quality employment continues to drive people to seek incapacity benefits support. So the State's spending on tax credits and incapacity benefits continues to undermine investment in competitiveness.

And despite the increase in the employment rate over the last ten years, at 74.7% (National Statistics) for the three months to November 2007, it is just below the rate it reached in 1972–75 and 1998–90 (Bivand, 2007). And despite 700,000 (17%) children being lifted out of poverty since 1998/99 (on the after housing cost figures), the government has missed its target of raising a quarter (one million) of the children out of poverty by March 2006 and progress is now stalling. The social exclusion task force is now concentrating on four groups who are victims of exclusion (prisoners, children in care, those with mental health problems and those with learning difficulties) rather than looking at the processes that exclude such groups in the first place.

We have argued that the tensions around competitiveness and collaboration have been addressed by trying to use collaboration to further competitiveness, but the tensions between sustainability and economic development have not been addressed at all. In the performance criteria set for RDAs and for local authority economic development there is no measure of sustainability. The climate change agenda and the economic development agenda run in parallel lines (Jones, 2007a) and if they meet economic development tends to dominate. The shifts in planning policy to facilitate major infrastructure investment, to respond to housing demand, to be demand-led and to favour development of all kinds, but most particularly, of course, for economic development, are evident.

The Brown Era and the Sub-national Review

Although Gordon Brown has not used the term 'the third way', one can anticipate a continuation of roll-out neoliberalism. The analysis of Gordon Brown's ideological stance has emphasised two aspects.

Firstly Gordon Brown has highlighted the superiority of the British reformist agenda with the emphasis on the individual and moral virtue (Lee, 2006) drawing on the work on Adam Smith who came from his home town. Matthew Watson (2007) has shown how Brown, in introducing asset based models of welfare and in his focus on social responsibility, draws on Smith's theory of moral sentiments, which focuses on how man can learn to live harmoniously and to flourish in a commercial society. But while Adam Smith argued that you need self command and moral tutoring to avoid self interest dominating in a market society, Brown argues that the self disciplining financial agent is pursuing their own self interest. He therefore individualises society's interest. But there is a contradiction in his approach. For assets to be profitable you need high returns: a rising stock exchange and rising house prices. Yet these high returns to assets increase inequalities and social exclusion and tie investment into rising land values rather than increasing productivity.

In addressing the problem of productivity Brown has directed policy to business growth and here lies his second ideological stance. As Stuart Hall argued above, his emphasis on the need to foster a dynamic economy and make markets more efficient has focused the function of government on delivery and an apparent politically neutral form of market managerialism. So while his use of Adam Smith leads to rhetoric about redistributing power from the state to the individual, his policy has in fact been centralising and technocratic. These tensions are evident in the Review of Sub-national Economic Development and Regeneration (SNR), 2007. The reforms proposed in the SNR and linked policy papers can be grouped into three categories.

Regional Governance Changes

The regional governance changes reveal strong centralisation even though this is being done in the name of greater accountability. This argument is dealt with in more detail in the viewpoint in this special issue by Tim Marshall, which focuses on the democratic deficit that is being created. Regional Assemblies are to go and planning and housing powers will be passed to Regional Development Agencies (RDAs) who will now be responsible for a single regional strategy by 2010. There is theoretically greater scrutiny of RDAs but this is meant to be led by leaders of councils on top of their day job of running the council and on top of the drivers for greater collaboration through MAA (13 sub-regional areas have been given the go ahead to negotiate MAAs by June 2008) and shared services. In the meantime there is no doubt about the centralisation of accountability. A Minister has been given responsibility for each region and there are likely to be Parliamentary Regional Select Committees (Maer & Parry, 2007).

Stronger Sub-regions to Deliver the Economic Agenda

RDAs are being tasked to delegate (not devolve) their budgets to sub-regional partnerships but only to do this where these partnerships can deliver on RDA targets. The key target is Gross Value Added (GVA) per hour worked – a productivity target linked to Brown's growth agenda that has no relationship to quality of life for residents (particularly as it is a workplace data set not related to where people live), sustainability or reducing inequality. The other RDA targets (employment rate, skills, Research and Development; business start up) are also strongly linked to a growth agenda.

So sub-regional economic development is meant to deliver economic growth. Some of the issues in delivering this agenda in areas with less competitive urban centres are highlighted in Ivan Turok's article in this special issue. It may be partly as a result of this tension that sub-regional and local action is being focused on worklessness, which is one of the local performance indicators (employment and worklessness; education and skills; investment in infrastructure; creating an attractive business environment and narrowing the gap), despite its absence from RDA targets. The worklessness agenda is rising up the political agenda and, as argued above, is a key tension in government policy where spending on incapacity benefits is seen as holding up investment in competitiveness. To reach the government's 80% employment rate it would be necessary to help a further one million Incapacity Benefit claimants into work, plus one million older workers and 300,000 lone parents. The new welfare to work regime will focus on this task and City Strategy Pathfinders funded by the DWP to join up services on worklessness are already active in 15 pathfinder areas. There is a move to merge funds and commissioning. Clause 4 in the Further Education and Training Bill gives the Mayor in

London the power of oversight and direction of LSC funds. This clause can be used by other regions to go to the Secretary of State and request similar powers. It is likely to figure in MAA proposals. One of the battles that will emerge in this new institutional space at the sub region is how to make the LSC, New Deal and Jobcentre Plus accountable to local partners and join up with local programmes and to monitor providers, including the third sector, rather than just deliver delegated programmes from RDAs and central government departments.

Local Government is being Asked to Take a Stronger Economic Development Role

Local authorities are being given significant new powers to encourage them to focus on economic development. This reflects the drive for growth mixed with the attempt to increase social responsibility, decrease worklessness and increase local entrepreneurship. These national drivers can only be delivered at the local level. Underpinning the new powers is a new duty on upper tier local authorities to do an economic assessment. There are major new responsibilities in the skills agenda. The school leaving age is currently being raised to 18 and there are proposals for funding of £7 billion for 14- to 19-year-olds to be devolved to local government.

Much of the agenda is to be clearly business-led. Local government will be encouraged to set up local employer-led skills and employment boards linking the skills and jobs agenda. They are being encouraged to set up city development companies and we have an *In Perspective* piece by Ian Bromley in this special issue on one of the first such companies in Sheffield. Employment Partnerships have involved 209 employers (January 2008 figure) in making job pledges and these now need to be implemented at the local level. Several have also made skill pledges which also need to be implemented locally. The LEGI funding (to promote entrepreneurialism in deprived areas will continue), as will Business Improvement Districts.

And to encourage growth and overcome reluctance to promote development, economic development is to be incentivised. The new financial instruments are linked more closely to economic development, growth and infrastructure development despite the reduction in LABGI (a payment to local authorities who achieve above target growth in business rates). Supplementary business rates are to be introduced and there is the new Community Infrastructure Levy (CIL) proposed in the Planning Bill; and on 4 December there was the announcement of the £732 million Growth Fund allocations are part of the Growth Areas and Growth Points programmes. PPS4 brings a stronger economic development focus to the planning agenda.

But government has still got an eye on mitigating the inequality that follows from a simple drive for business growth. Neighbourhood

Renewal Funding is to become the Working Neighbourhood Fund (WNF) with £2 billion funding to some 50 local authorities. The DWP deprived areas fund in City Strategy Pathfinder areas is being aligned with the new WNF (see DWP website: http://www.dwp.gov.uk/welfarereform/support_pathfinders.asp).

All these changes are likely to be in place by 2010/2011. So far a few local authorities have grappled with City Strategy Pathfinders and many, both in and outside the pathfinder areas, are not aware of or engaged in this programme. The agenda above calls for skills in economic assessments, skills in linking the neighbourhood agenda and worklessness; skills in negotiating with business, skills in drawing together complex funding streams and programmes, an understanding of the skills and employment agenda and how these can be brought together, project appraisal and management and an understanding of the levers and drivers of the local authority and its partners. Money is being given to the Regional Improvement and Efficiency Partnerships to build capacity but there remain concerns about the scale of the task. If local economic development cannot rise to the challenge it is clear that the RDAs and business agenda will dominate delivery. The viewpoint by Tim Marshall in this issue reflects this concern. So what is the future of LED? It is to this we now turn.

The Future of Economic Development

This article has emphasised the dominance of the neoliberal agenda within the future of local economic development. But this does not mean that local economic development officers will have to reinforce this trend. As Doreen Massey argues:

> 'Neoliberalism' is sometimes written about as though there is an automatic transmission belt from some ethereal sphere of greater forces to 'how it plays out on the ground'. It is not so. There are indeed pressures and constraints, often of immense power but there are also agents who play along, or resist, or struggle mightily. There is room for political intervention. (Massey, 2007, p.30)

The three articles in this special issue also identify the opportunities and scope for optimism.

Firstly, as Turok argues, the whole place-shaping agenda and duty to carry out an economic assessment provide an important basis for ensuring that economic development is not just business-led. Local authorities will want to involve residents in their place shaping and can choose to enhance the less powerful voices that address the wider impact on the business growth agenda. Presenting business with information about environmental issues, worklessness, low pay and job churn, the congestion implications of not linking place making and local job access etc can in itself provide a strong challenge to a pure neo liberal agenda. Graham Haughton and Phil Allmendinger argue that local economic development officers need to hold out for performance targets and evaluation frameworks that reflect this wider view of economic development. Doreen Massey (2007, p. 32) would like to see the debate about place shaping going even further and not only addressing how to undermine the constraints of the global economy in the interests of local residents but also challenging the way large global cities reinforce those global neo liberal inequalities on other less competitive urban centres: 'This means, for example, not only tackling the causes of inequality and climate change in London, but also taking responsibility for its role in producing these problems worldwide.'

Secondly Alex Nunn and Steve Johnson welcome the rhetoric of integrating the employment and skills systems and argue that it will be a key challenge for local economic development to turn this into a reality and one that provides genuine help to break the 'no pay–low pay' cycle of poverty. This new agenda and increased flexibility in employment programmes has also been welcomed by Inclusion (Simmonds, 2007) arguing that the increased 'work-first' approach will need to be balanced with new measures to improve retention bringing together a number of different agencies and funding stream all acting on different parts of the system.

This brings us to the third area of opportunity, the institutional reform. On the one hand there is the increased centralisation driven by the RDAs and their performance targets. However, there is also an emphasis on the local and sub-regional as the only arena where these different agencies and funding streams can be pulled together to meet the needs of specific individuals and local communities. The new focus on local economic development is widely welcomed by the practitioners who have written for *In Perspective* in this special issue. Graham Haughton and Phil Allmendinger suggest that the new 'soft spaces', with functional rather than administrative boundaries, provide considerable opportunity. They see the economic development officer as a broker playing a key role in the way in which different types of relationships are constructed and conducted across variable geographies. The extent to which local priorities are given space in these new relationships is still open to negotiation.

Graham Haughton and Phil Allmendinger also see a growing importance for liveability issues, the 'soft infrastructure' and this brings us back to the sustainability and economic development agenda. Just because the government has failed to join up these two agenda it does not mean that they cannot be joined up locally. Volume 22 Issue 1 of *Local Economy* on the environment and local economic development contained a set of articles and *In Perspective* case studies showing precisely how these two agendas can be brought together. Jackson (2007) looked at using strategic environmental assessment to deliver sustainable local development. Subsequently Jones (2007b) has published a very useful and thoughtful article, *Greening Growth*, which argues for constructing a system of integrated environmental and economic accounts. It calls on local authorities to widen the duty to produce an economic assessment to include an inventory of local environmental assets. The proposed benefits, in monetary terms, of any development could then be set against any environmental costs, also expressed in monetary terms.

While the government's neoliberal agenda will limit what can be achieved, the new focus on local economic development opens up some opportunities. Local authorities continue to have a number of levers they can pull in influencing this agenda. They are the legitimate representatives of the local community and can ensure all voices are heard and policy is not simply business-led. They are meant to scrutinise the RDAs. They can influence the shape and agenda of local networks and partnerships and how they are going to assess their effectiveness. They have planning powers; influence over transport provision; can influence local job quality through procurement and commissioning; can work with employers to deliver locally the national skill and job pledges; they will have significant influence on the skills agenda; and, with the local hospital, they are usually the biggest employer in the area. They have the potential to bring the place shaping agenda together with the employment and skills agenda in a positive framework that will bring real benefits to local people. This is the challenge that faces the future of local economic development.

References

Bivand, P. (2007) Why is the employment rate falling?, *Working Brief*, 188(Oct.), pp. 16–18.

Brenner, N. & Theodore, N. (2002) (Eds) *Spaces of Neoliberalism: Urban Restructuring in North America and Western Europe* (Oxford: Blackwell).

Dorling, D., Rigby, J., Wheeler, B., Ballas, D., Thomas, B., Fahmy, E., Gordon, D. & Lupton, R. (2007) *Poverty, Wealth and Place in Britain 1968 to 2005* (Bristol: Policy Press).

Finlayson, A. (2003) *Making Sense of New Labour* (London: Lawrence and Wishart).

Fuller, C. & Geddes, M. (forthcoming 2008) Urban governance under neo-liberalism: New Labour and the restructuring of state-space, *Antipode*.

Geddes, M. & Newman, I. (1999) Evolution and conflict in local economic development, *Local Economy*, 14(1), pp. 12–26.

Giddens, A. (2004) Did they foul up any third way? *New Statesman*, 7 June. http://www.newstatesman.com/200406070017.

Hall, S. (2007) Will life after Blair be different?, *British Politics*, 2, pp. 118–122.

HM Treasury, Department for Business, Enterprise and Regulatory Reform, and Communities and Local Government (2007) *Review of Sub-national Economic Development and Regeneration* (London: HM Treasury, BERR, CLG).

Jackson, T. (2007) Mainstreaming sustainability in local economic development practice, *Local Economy*, 22(1), pp. 12–26.

Jones, A. (2007a) Counting the cost of living, *New Start*, 9(410), p. 18.

Jones, A. (2007b) *Greening Growth: How Local Government can Build the Green Economy* (London: Local Government Information Unit).

Lee, S. (2006) Gordon Brown and the British way, *Political Quarterly*, 77(3), pp. 369–378.

Maer, L. & Parry, K. (2007) *The Proposed Regional Select Committees and the Future of Regional Assemblies*, Standard Note SN/PC/4411 (London: Parliament and Constitution Centre, House of Commons Library).

Massey, D. (2007) A new politics of space, *Red Pepper*, Aug./Sept., pp. 30–32.

Palmer, G., MacInnes, T. & Kenway, P. (2007) *Monitoring Poverty and Social Exclusion 2007* (York: Joseph Rowntree Foundation).

Peck, J. & Tickell, A. (2002) Neoliberalising space, in: N. Brenner & N. Theodore (Eds) *Spaces of Neoliberalism: Urban Restructuring in North America and Western Europe*, pp. 33–37 (Oxford: Blackwell).

Simmonds, D. (2007) 'In work, better off' – is both right and wrong, *Working Brief*, 188(Oct.), pp. 3–7.

Watson, M. (2007) Paper presented at a seminar on Labour and Planning organised by Tim Marshall and Andy Inch at Oxford Brookes University. Event Programme available at http://www.pnuk.org.uk/newlabour.htm (forthcoming in *Planning Practice and Research*).

Wilks-Heeg, S. (2007) Paper presented at a seminar on Labour and Planning organised by Tim Marshall and Andy Inch at Oxford Brookes University. Event Programme availabe at http://www.pnuk.org/newlabour.htm (*forthcoming in Planning Practice and Research*).

FEATURES

Labouring and Learning towards Competitiveness: The Future of Local Labour Markets after Harker, Leitch and Freud

ALEX NUNN & STEVE JOHNSON

ABSTRACT In 1999 Geddes and Newman highlighted five key tensions in New Labour's adoption of the 'new centrist' approach to Local Economic Development (LED). This article reflects on the continuing relevance of these tensions in relation local labour markets and in the light of the publication of three major independent reviews of policy in relation to child poverty, skills provision and welfare reform and the Government's response to these. It suggests that in the main the tensions identified by Geddes and Newman remain relevant, especially within the emerging national policy framework. However, it also ends optimistically, by suggesting that there is scope for LED actors to piece together an approach which can begin to move toward a resolution of the tensions through bringing together employment and skills policies at the local level, developing more effective models of partnership working (including with employers), and taking the sustainability agenda more seriously.

Introduction

This article reflects on the progress of the New Labour government in relation to local economic development, and in particular on the organisation, structure and political economy of labour markets. The publication of several important policy reviews and responses from government during 2006 and 2007 offers a strong basis for comparison of the last ten years of social and labour market reform, setting out the likely future trajectory of policy and practice in relation to labour markets under the then new government headed by Gordon Brown. Geddes and Newman's (1999) article in this journal provides a useful structure for organizing this comparison. The five key tensions they identified shortly after New Labour came to power in 1997 retain their validity in relation to understanding contemporary and future policies in relation to local economic development.

This article charts briefly the development of labour market policy over the period 1997–2007 using this 'five tensions' framework. It then goes on to use the same framework to review critically three key sets of policy documents in relation to child poverty (DWP, 2007b; Harker, 2006), skills (Department for Innovation Universities and Skills–DIUS, 2007; Leitch, 2006) and welfare reform (DWP, 2007a; Freud, 2007) and sets out some conclusions regarding the future of local labour markets and the implications for local economic development.

Geddes and Newman's five tensions

Geddes and Newman (1999) summarised the debate in Local Economic Development (LED) over the preceding two decades, charting several shifts and patterns in LED, from the social democratic post-war model to the New Right policies of the Conservatives in the 1980s and early 1990s. Writing immediately following the election of the New Labour government in 1997, Geddes and Newman looked forward, to identify with remarkable clarity, five key tensions that lay at the heart of the approach that they described as the 'new centrism'. First – competitiveness and collaboration – highlighted the tension between New Labour's continued adherence to neoliberal principles of competitiveness with their acknowledgement of the apparent need to shift toward partnerships and network governance (Newman, 2005; Piore & Sabel, 1984; Rhodes, 1996, 1997).

Second was the tension between commitments to labour market flexibility alongside the emphasis on improving the quality of employment. Third was a possible tension between initiatives to create jobs and concerns about the wider social effects of poor quality employment and the environmental impacts of low-grade economic development. Fourth was the accepted need to knit together contrasting interests in the public, private and third sectors through state agency and in support of state-led socioeconomic goals, such as regeneration. Finally, they identified the contradictory implications of efforts to pursue sustainable development on the one hand and economic growth on the other.

Given these tensions, Geddes and Newman (1999) posited three potential future scenarios for LED: (1) a 'muddling through' within the parameters of the new centrism, while leaving the five tensions unresolved; (2) a 'triple squeeze' scenario in which pressures from Europe, central government and the new regional institutions would 'submerge local economic development in an ever more amorphous "regeneration" policy' (p. 23); and (3) harnessing emerging social concerns with the failure of neoliberal capitalism, around a rejuvenated European Social Model (ESM) or increasingly visible environmental problems, to substantively confront and resolve the five tensions, principally in the form of elevating social justice over competitiveness as a core concern.

Labour Market Policy Since 1999

This article argues that labour market policy developments since Geddes and Newman's (1999) article offer evidence that aspects of all three of these potential scenarios have in fact played out. Certainly, the five tensions have continued to be present in labour market reform pursued under the New Labour Project (NLP). However, the NLP has neither confronted these nor muddled through (as the first scenario would suggest). 'Muddling through' would imply that no balance or resolution had been attempted (whether ultimately achieved or not) between the tensions identified. The third scenario would suggest that policy objectives of competitiveness had been subjugated to social justice when in fact the opposite has been true, with social justice most often defined as a path toward competitiveness. Finally, while concerns with local economic development have not disappeared under institutional anarchy, as the second scenario might have it, the waters have at times been significantly muddied by institutional proliferation and confusion over the location of policy and implementation responsibility between and within different levels of governance.

Labour market reform within the NLP has been advanced most notably through the government's Welfare to Work strategy and various initiatives to promote enhanced productivity through improving the skills base. Welfare to Work policy has focused on three key issues: promoting work as the most effective route out of poverty, 'making work pay' through the minimum wage and various tax credit regimes and addressing inactivity and long-term exclusion from the labour market through both national welfare regimes and locally targeted Area Based Initiatives (ABIs).

Widening access to employment opportunity has been pursued through a range of 'active labour market' policies (ALMPs) (HM Treasury, 1999), including the various New Deals targeted at specific demographic groups identified as being overrepresented among the unemployed (Dickens *et al.*, 2000; Finn, 2003, p. 712; HM Treasury, 2002; Office of Public Sector, 2002; Sector Skills Development Agency–SSDA, 2003b, p. 7). National programmes to enhance 'employability' have been augmented by various geographically targeted programmes such as Working Neighbourhoods Pilots (Dewson, 2005, p. 14), Employment Zones and Action Teams, where the focus has often been to transform not just individual employability, but the culture of whole communities toward employment. Across all initiatives, the approach has included employment and job-search advice, work-focused training and assistance and help with some of the costs associated with starting work. While there are these strong common themes in the packages of support on offer, the sheer proliferation of agencies, contractors and local models provides some evidence of institutional confusion and ambiguity over where responsibility for policy and practice lie.

A continuing theme of the Welfare to Work strategy has been to concentrate support on those facing the most serious barriers to employment as a means of overcoming long-term unemployment, inactivity and 'worklessness'.[1] The 2006 Welfare Reform Bill, with the roll-out of the Pathways to Work initiative suggests an intensification of this approach (DWP, 2006). While tackling long-term unemployment clearly has a social justice rationale, it is also notable that policy concerns with short-term frictional unemployment are less pronounced, with the latter seen as a necessary part of the functioning of a competitive labour market. The implication of this is that the third of Geddes and Newman's scenarios has not arisen precisely because the NLP has promoted social justice not as a factor overriding concerns with competitiveness but primarily as a pathway to competitiveness (Cammack, 2007; Jessop, 2007; Nunn, 2006, 2007). It is interesting to note that this increasing focus on targeting excluded groups arose as the labour market came closer and closer to 'full employment', suggesting that economic competitiveness rather than social justice *per se* has been central to the concerns of policy makers. In this context, the benefits of work for the individual and for poor families are stressed much more forcefully than are the negative impacts of poor quality or insecure employment and cyclical returns to benefit dependency.[2]

In parallel with Welfare to Work policies a raft of policies and interventions have attempted to enhance the skills base of the workforce, with the principal aim of increasing productivity and competitiveness:

> British business can no longer compete on the basis of low cost, low value added activity. To be successful, it is even more important for business and individuals to learn new skills, be more creative and innovative and use their knowledge to produce higher value added goods and services. (DFEE and DTI, 2001)

Substantial spending increases on education have signified the commitment to this agenda. Spending has been matched by efforts to reform the curriculum with a tighter focus on basic and transferable skills and, at the local level, making linkages with employers, though not necessarily always successfully (see Hallgarten & Watling, 2001), in special initiatives like Education Action Zones (EAZs), Excellence in Cities

---

[1] See for instance: Corden *et al.* (2005, p. 85); Dewson (2005); Griffiths *et al.* (2006); Hirst *et al.* (2006); Knight *et al.* (2005); Policy Research Institute (2006).

[2] For instance see references in ministerial speeches and Freud (2007, p. 5) to Waddell and Burton (2006), which reviews evidence of the links between work and well-being. While Waddell and Burton find overwhelming evidence of the benefits of employment for heath, they are also clear that this needs to be good quality employment and to fit the individual's health requirements.

and City Academy programmes (Centre for Public Services, 2003, pp. 21–24). Efforts have also been made to strengthen the linkages between education and enterprise against a background analysis that competitive pressures necessitate a greater emphasis on entrepreneurial skills and flexible behaviour in the school curriculum in the future (e.g. Davies, 2002).

Skills policy generally has also been placed in this context, again stressing the importance of brokering economic inclusion within the labour market as a pathway to competitiveness. A key concern here is to reform skills provision to match the skills needs of employers, demonstrated by the vast array of skills studies and strategies being produced at national, regional and local level (DfES, 2003b; Leitch, 2006; Low Pay Commission, 2003; SSDA, 2003a, 2003b). The NLP has also driven the establishment of a variety of institutional structures to promote the improvement of skills in both the active and latent workforce, most notably the sector based Skills for Business Network of Sector Skills Councils and the Sector Skills Development Agency (to be subsumed into the Commission for Employment and Skills after barely five years of operation). Again this tends to suggest that institutional proliferation may have led to some confusion about the location of policy and practice responsibilities.

The policy trajectory with regard to labour markets since Geddes and Newman put forward their three possible future scenarios in 1999 suggests that there is little evidence of the third: challenging the hegemonic discourse of competitiveness in the global economy as a means of resolving the five tensions they highlight from within the parameters of a renewed European Social Model. While there is evidence of a balancing the contradictory concerns set out in the five tensions, this is not necessarily an unreflective 'muddling through'. Rather it may be seen as a conscious strategy of holding these in tension. For instance, while competitiveness remains the key *telos* of labour market policy, there is a clear recognition of the acceptance of a need to generate webs of governance at a local, regional and national level to pursue this. In particular, this has been pursued through the use of common outcome-based targets, for instance in the form of the Regional Development Agency target framework and more recently in the form of Local Area Agreements (LAAs) and Multi-Area Agreements (MAAs), which have often stressed issues of competitiveness.

There have been noticeable attempts to tie together a complex alliance of public, private and third sector actors within this 'network' of governance through membership of boards and forums facilitated by RDAs, Regional Assemblies, local LSCs, Local Strategic Partnerships and special local regeneration vehicles. On the second and third tensions – those connected to the trade-off between the quantity and quality of jobs – a balance has again been attempted, though with the emphasis being more toward the competitiveness concern rather than social justice. While the quality and social impact of employment are recognised in policy this is often seen first and foremost as a means of facilitating competitiveness. The final tension between growth and sustainability has attracted rhetorical acknowledgement without any clear indication of political (or indeed wider 'popular') willingness to sacrifice a preoccupation with economic growth to achieve this. So far the discussions of what implications a radical sustainable development strategy might have for local labour markets (such as, for instance, attempts to control or encourage shorter travel to work distances) have been limited, though consideration of these issues is now developing rapidly (e.g. Jones & Ennis, 2007; Stern, 2006).

The preceding discussion implicitly provides evidence for the institutional proliferation which has at times threatened to swamp LED within a web of organisational complexity. This is true in terms of looking upwards at the institutional channels between the local level and central government, especially in relation to labour markets where the Learning and Skills Councils, Sector Skills Councils, Regional Development Agencies, Jobcentre Plus and Local Authorities all appear to have some form of policy remit and all have different organisational status and linkages with different central government departments. On top of this, the local level has seen the proliferation of ABIs, some semipermanent, others with strict and defined time limits but almost all introducing new layers of complexity and confusion. This corresponds in many ways to the new – or polycentric – governance image which is part and parcel of the shift to networks and collaboration but is noted to herald a confusing web of actors with differing but overlapping spatial and policy remits (Hooghe & Marks, 2001a, 2001b).

Future Tensions and Challenges

Harker, Leitch and Freud

During late 2006 and 2007 three major 'independent' reviews of government policy were published which, together with their associated responses from central government mark a watershed in labour market policy under New Labour. This is so for several reasons, including the close association of those reviews published while Tony Blair was still Prime Minister, with the policy areas of skills, competitiveness and child poverty dominated by Gordon Brown as Chancellor and because the government's responses to them have been closely correlated with the Prime Ministerial shift. Taken together the Harker Review of Child Poverty (2006), the Leitch Review of Skills (2006) and the Freud Review of Welfare Reform (2007) and the government's responses to them offer a glimpse of the newly emerging second phase in the New Labour Project of social and economic reform.

All three sets of documents set out to problematise a particular social issue in relation to their particular policy remit. For Harker (2006) this is continuing levels of child poverty despite progress toward getting more families with children into employment. She thus focuses on the need to support working families to find good quality work, to stay in work and to progress in the labour market. The Leitch (2006) review of skills focuses on the competitive threat posed by emerging market economies and domestic demographic change and argues strongly that up-skilling the workforce to move the UK economy higher up the global division of labour is the only way to succeed socially and economically in this context. Freud (2006) argues that while progress has been made in tackling unemployment, more needs to be done to combat long-term inactivity, complex and multiple barriers to work.

Taken together, the government's responses to these reviews (DIUS, 2007; DWP, 2007a, 2007b) broadly accept their general conclusions. They suggest a programme of reform based on streamlining the benefits system, rationalising skills governance and improving delivery through 'employer-led' approaches and developing greater linkages between the skills and welfare systems, through the creation of the Commission for Employment and Skills, Local Employment and Skills Boards, Local Employment Partnerships and the agreement of both Jobs and Skills Pledges between public agencies and employers.

Competitiveness or Collaboration

We have argued that a concern to secure competitiveness forms the essential rationale for the vast majority of New Labour policies in relation to labour markets. In fact the 1997 election manifesto made it clear that the NLP would not seek to challenge the notion of competitive pressures emerging from globalisation but to work within this framework to promote enhanced competitiveness as a means of coping with it (Labour Party, 1997). The Leitch, Harker and Freud reports all strongly align themselves with this vision of the need to enhance competitiveness not just to cope with the challenge of existing competitors in Europe and North America, but also most notably from emerging market economies such as China and India:

> The UK's challenge is to drive greater increases in prosperity as the global economy changes fundamentally . . . Technology is rapidly breaking down the barriers between what can and cannot be traded. All work than can be digitalised, automated, and outsourced can increasingly be done by the most effective and competitive individuals or enterprises, wherever they are located. (Leitch, 2006, p. 7)

This widely shared competitiveness goal does not appear to current policy makers, as it did to Geddes and Newman, to lay in tension with the need to broker collaboration through new forms of governance precisely because it is so widely shared. Among the wide network of institutions charged with delivering elements of labour market policy, there is an almost universal commitment to the goals of facilitating competitiveness. Indeed, network governance has been widely used as a means to secure broad-based consensus, with the participation of 'economic and social partners' now widely practised at a local and regional level in relation to LED and labour market initiatives specifically. This again underlies the major innovations that emerge collectively from Leitch, Harker and Freud. Notwithstanding the identification of a degree of institutional complexity and the need for simplification in Leitch (2006, pp. 71–85), coalitions of interested parties are to be brokered nationally through the Commission for Employment and Skills. Interestingly these coalitions aim, first, to provide a forum for 'joined up' government within the public sector between the devolved administrations of the UK, between different central government departments, between central government and its agencies and between the agencies themselves. Second, it is intended to incorporate other parties outside governance: principally employers but also, as a junior partner, Trade Unions (DIUS, 2007, p. 38; Leitch, 2006, p. 77).

This approach is then to be replicated at a local level through the Employment and Skills Boards, already announced in the Local Government White Paper (DCLG, 2006) and Local Employment Partnerships, announced in the 2006 Budget (HM Treasury, 2006). Further, employer led measures continue to be promoted through revised Sector Skills Councils and Agreements (DIUS, 2007, pp. 39–50). The aim of the new local level infrastructure proposed by both the Leitch Implementation plan and the Welfare green paper (DWP, 2007b, pp. 31–37, 52–54) is also to attempt to utilise network governance to facilitate greater linkages between the employment and skills agenda[3], as recommended by Harker (pp. 38–42) and Leitch (pp. 120–129) in particular.

The point here is that collaboration, through network forms of 'new' governance, is securely anchored as the preferred means of implementing policies, programmes and initiatives which are designed to pursue the underlying objective of competitiveness. While there are clearly aspects of coping with institutional proliferation and ambiguity, this is neither 'muddling through' or a resolution of the tension between competitiveness and collaboration in favour of a renewed European Social Model and rejection of neoliberalism. Rather, it is a political project aimed at securing widespread institutional support to implement measures designed to promote competitiveness.

Flexible Labour Markets or Good Employers

Tensions between labour market flexibility and the quality of employment also remain. The Harker review takes a strong stance on this point, stressing the need to combat in-work poverty and frequent transitions between unemployment and low paid work. Harker (pp. 36–42) is thus

[3] For example through the Jobs and Skills Pledges.

clear that more needs to be done to ensure that lone parents and adults in families with children are able to find employment of suitable quality or that they are supported to progress from 'entry' level work and that this will require some integration of welfare to work, careers advice and skills provision at a local level. Here the Jobs Pledge promised for Local Employment Partnerships in the Welfare Green Paper (pp. 32–37) and the Skills Pledge proposed in the Leitch implementation report (pp. 53–58) appear also to recognise the importance of generating employer commitment to enhanced quality of employment outcomes for job seekers.

However, these developments again do not so much seek to resolve the tension between flexible labour markets and quality employment. Rather they hold this in tension, fully committing to the competitiveness and flexibility agenda but attempting to design policy interventions and local institutional frameworks which can cope with the potentially negative social impacts of flexibility. As such, the quality of employment is not to be improved through regulation but through competitiveness itself. The policy logic runs that if only the labour force is skilled enough, and employers can be persuaded of the advantages of enhancing their productivity through training their existing workforce, the position of UK employers within the global division of labour can be enhanced and better quality employment will ensue in any case:

> increasingly, skills are a key determinant of employment . . . In the new global economy, people's security will not depend on trying to protect particular jobs, holding back the tide of change. It is not enough to rely on the traditional model of protecting people from change. Instead the best form of welfare will be to ensure people can find their next job, staying in the labour market. The best way to do this is to ensure that have a basic platform of skills that allows flexibility and can update their skills as the economy changes. (Leitch, 2006, p. 3)
>
> The openness and flexibility of the UK economy has presented labour market opportunities for many individuals. It has also created specific challenges for individuals with no or low skills. The global market is expanding at an unprecedented rate and parts of the economy, particularly the service economy, are likely to be exposed to international competition to an extent that they have not been before. In short, in an increasingly global economy a failure to tackle low skills could damage the UK's competitiveness and entrench poverty. (Freud, 2007, p. 26)

This approach is broadly consistent with the 'flexicurity' approach promoted through the European Employment Strategy which emphasises 'employment' security rather than 'job' security (European Commission, 2007; Haahr & Andersen, 2006). Rather than to regulate flexible labour markets it seeks to ensure continuing opportunities for employment through competitiveness and attracting investment and labour demand. As such it is fully in line with an evolved 'new centrism' which is now widely accepted, at least in principle, throughout Western Europe (e.g. Wilthagen, 2007).

If the apparent contradiction between flexibility and good quality employment is to be successfully held in tension, much hinges on implementation at the local level. It will be crucial for those involved in LED through local governance initiatives to ensure that continuities in service are maintained to ensure employment security and progression.

Jobs or Social Inclusion

The 'work first' mantra – the notion that 'work is the best route out of poverty' – pervades New Labour statements about labour market and social policies. The change of Prime Minister in 2007 appears to have made little difference to this, as indicated by the July 2007 Green Paper *In Work, Better Off* (DWP, 2007a):

> the chance to work opens up the chance to progress, to develop and to participate fully in society. (DWP, 2007, p. 25)

As Geddes and Newman pointed out in 1999, there are inherent tensions within the 'work first' notion. There is scant empirical evidence to support the idea that encouraging workless people to enter any type of employment, however low-paid or insecure, leads in some automatic or predictable way to reduced levels of poverty for individuals, families or communities and Harker is clear that the in-work poverty remains an important problem (2006, p. 38). Indeed, it can be argued that regeneration initiatives at the local level based on this approach can aggravate socioeconomic divisions through, for example, increased property prices, changed commuting patterns favouring car owners and the closure of community facilities such as local shops. Furthermore, little of the wealth created through such regeneration initiatives may be recycled into deprived communities.

A central missing link in New Labour policies has been the relationship between 'work first' policies on the one hand, ostensibly concerned with poverty reduction and social inclusion, and competitiveness-oriented skills policies on the other. The almost simultaneous publication of the Welfare to Work Green Paper and the Leitch Review Implementation Report (DIUS, 2007) provided a major opportunity for the Government to spell out how employment and skills policies might be integrated in order to achieve the dual objectives of competitiveness and social inclusion. This is particularly important given the current congestion in the 'entry' level jobs market even without the influx of economic migrants from the Accession States of the European Union.

The Green Paper states that 'the system must do more to help people stay in work and move up the ladder' (DWP, 2007b, p. 9). The Leitch Implementation Report envisages a 'joined up employment and skills system' (DIUS, 2007, p. 10). The overall impression is, however, of a lack of clarity regarding the links between the employment and skills agendas. For instance, neither paper explicitly makes the link between the Jobs and

Skills Pledges that might act as an occupational escalator out of poverty, especially where significant local employers are signed up to the whole package. The absence of this is doubly concerning given the apparent policy confusion suggested by the failure to address the local economic development and labour market implications of recent patterns of economic migration and the impact of this in terms of depressing wages and abuses of worker rights.

A key challenge for local economic development will be to work with the new policy agenda and the new institutional framework (notably the proposed Commission for Employment and Skills and Local Employment Partnerships) to ensure that the rhetoric of an integrated employment and skills system is turned into a reality, and one that provides genuine help for individuals and communities to break the 'no pay–low pay' cycle of poverty while at the same time developing workforce skills as one contributor to improving the competitiveness of local economies. This will need to reflect the need to increase social inclusion for recent migrant communities as well as more settled social groups.

Public, Private or Third Sector Provision

'Partnership' is central to both the welfare to work and skills agendas. Indeed two chapters of the Welfare to Work White Paper are devoted to the topic. 'Local Employment Partnerships' are envisaged, with involvement from employers such as Asda, B&Q and Tesco, focused primarily on the 'economic advantages of employing a diverse workforce'. These appear to be a development of the Local Employer Coalitions established by the National Employment Panel to give employers a greater influence over welfare to work initiatives at the local level. In return for employer involvement, 'we will guarantee that job applicants will have the right attitude to work as well as the right aptitude'. The suggestion here is of a rather unequal partnership in which large employers decide what types of 'attitude' are required and government and providers undertake to somehow 'guarantee' that these will be forthcoming. There appears to be little suggestion of employers being encouraged to rethink their requirements or to redesign jobs or training programmes in order to provide opportunities for those at a disadvantage in the labour market.

The dominance of employer interests within 'partnership' approaches to employment and skills policies is further emphasised in the Leitch Implementation Report. While the proposed 'demand-led' approach to skills mentions both employers and learners, it is clear from the detailed proposals that the idea of 'employers leading the way on skills' is central to the New Labour conception of skills policies:

> we will give employers the opportunity to exert real leverage and decision-making over both the content and delivery of skills and employment programmes . . . We will . . . create a new UK Commission for Employment and

> Skills that will . . . strengthen the employer voice at the heart of the system. (DIUS, 2007, p. 11)

The report sets out potential roles for providers, further and higher education institutions and trade unions. It is clear, however, that these are seen as secondary to the dominant role of employers in the 'demand-led' system. Local Employment Partnerships are also mentioned, but with no clear or explicit link to the central Leitch agenda of developing 'World Class Skills'. In addition, and with no apparent link to the Local Employment Partnerships, the Commission for Employment and Skills will support 'a new network of local employer-led Employment and Skills Boards' (ESBs; DIUS, 2007, p. 44). The ESBs will, for example, be expected to play a role in local regeneration projects and major initiatives such as the 2012 Olympics.

The complexity of the local institutional landscape in relation to employment and skills is acknowledged in the statement that 'one goal should be to simplify the range of existing local bodies' (DIUS, 2007, p. 45) and the suggestion that local area agreements might be linked to the newly created (or restructured) organisations. It is hard to escape the conclusion, however, that the implementation of both the Welfare to Work and Leitch reports is likely to lead to further institutional complexity and pose challenges for groups wishing to influence the implementation of skills and employment policies at the local level.

A further complicating factor is the potential role of the 'third sector', particularly in relation to employment policies. New Labour's wider philosophy (see for example Department of Trade and Industry, 2002) puts voluntary and community sector organisations, and increasingly 'social enterprises', at the heart of the delivery of a range of social policies, and this approach has been evident particularly in relation to welfare to work. Third sector organisations are central to the delivery of New Deal and 'enhanced New Deal' initiatives such as the Employment Zones (Policy Research Institute, 2006). Such approaches pose a real dilemma for many organisations. Their financial survival is increasingly dependent on the winning of government contracts with often stringent performance criteria attached. To that extent they may find themselves increasingly 'sucked in' to the delivery of interventions that they may feel do not necessarily benefit their client groups. This in turn may affect their ability to act as independent voices in local, regional and national partnership processes and calls into question the potential of at least some parts of the 'third sector' to contribute towards genuinely community-based initiatives to address poverty and worklessness.

Sustainable Development or Economic Growth

The issue of sustainable economic development a local, national and global levels has risen up the policy agenda since Geddes and Newman's 1999 article and the establishment of the Academy for Sustainable

Communities in 2005 reflects the skills dimension of the sustainability agenda, particularly among professionals and others that are involved in the local development process. Moreover, the publication of the Stern Review into the economics of climate change has initiated further debate on the labour market and skills implications of future sustainability imperatives. Interestingly then, neither the Leitch report nor the Welfare to Work White Paper make more than passing reference to sustainability or the skills required to support the development of sustainable communities at the local level. To an extent this reflects the fact that the Department for Communities and Local Government has had limited involvement in the employment and skills agenda. However, it may also reflect a relatively short-term focus on economic competitiveness and a relatively narrow view of the skills required to achieve such competitiveness. Local economic development actors have a key role in ensure that the important generic skills identified by the Egan Review (2004) are reflected – at the local level at least – in the employment and skills agenda, emphasising a much wider view of the concept of competitiveness that results in sustainable improvements in the quality of life for local communities. This is very briefly acknowledged in the preface to the Leitch Implementation Plan (DIUS, 2007, p. 4):

> As the Stern Review set out in compelling terms, we will not secure the future we all want for our nation, indeed for our planet, if we do not reflect on our responsibility to the environment in all that we do. We need to ensure that we have the skills necessary to protect and improve the environment we live and work in.

However, this is not picked up as a substantive theme in the remainder of the document save for a seven-line paragraph at the end of the first chapter, which reads as an afterthought and simply reasserts that sustainability needs to be at the 'heart of our skills provision' (p. 20) without clearly explaining what precisely this means or how it is to be achieved.

Conclusions

A brief review of the current trajectory of reforms, as set out in the Harker, Leitch and Freud reviews and the response of central government to them, suggests that the five tensions outlined by Geddes and Newman in 1999 remain important, especially at national level. In relation to the first of these, the apparent tension between the need to embed competitiveness and collaborative governance systems, the tension appears to have been largely resolved for the time being, as a result of the widespread acceptance of the overall competitiveness goal which is rarely seriously questioned. There is less evidence of a resolution to the tensions related to competitiveness and economic growth on the one hand and social and environmental goals on the other. Rather, the preceding discussion suggests that there is, at best, ambiguity about the sincerity that can be attached to the central government commitment to the second half of this equation, with competitiveness and growth most often appearing to be the *main*, if not (quite) the *only*, show in town.

By contrast environmental sustainability, at least on the evidence provided by current national policy frameworks in relation to labour markets, is a rather tangential concern. Social inclusion and good quality employment fare a little better. But there remains uncertainty whether the 'work first' approach can deliver genuine social inclusion in the long term or whether the increased emphasis, most notably in the Harker Review, on broadening this approach to have a more inclusive and solidaristic tendency, is either sufficient or genuine enough to lead to substantive change.

However, two characteristics in the policy trajectory sketched out in these six documents offers some scope for optimism about the space available to local actors to resolve Geddes and Newman's remaining four tensions. This is the case first because the emphasis on local (whether at regional, local authority or 'city-region' level) institutional capacity building and limited autonomy in relation to intervention design and emphasis may create the institutional and organisational framework to address these issues. Second, the mere acknowledgement of the importance of a 'work first plus' approach and the need to link skills and welfare provision more closely together, whether rhetorical or otherwise, creates the political and policy space for local actors to legitimately confront the remaining tensions. As such, while there may be a case for continuing scepticism regarding the national policy framework, there may be scope for LED actors to at least try to reconcile some of the tensions to the benefit of their communities, for instance through bringing together employment and skills policies at the local level, developing more effective models of partnership working (including with employers), and taking the sustainability agenda more seriously.

References

Cammack, P. (2007) Competitiveness, social justice and the third way, *Papers in the Politics of Global Competitiveness*, 6, pp. 1–20.

Centre for Public Services (2003) Mortgaging Our Children's Future (Sheffield: CPS).

Corden, A., Nice, K. & Sainsbury, R. (2005) *Incapacity Reforms Pilot: Findings from a longitudinal panel of clients*. Department for Work and Pensions Research Report 259 (London: DWP). Available at: http://www.dwp.gov.uk/asd/asd5/rports2005-2006/rrep259.pdf

Davies, H. (2002) *A Review of Enterprise and the Economy in Education* (London: HM Treasury) February. Available at http://www.dfes.gov.uk/ebnet/download/Review.pdf

Department for Communities and Local Government (2006) *Strong and Prosperous Communities: The Local Government White Paper*, CM6939 (London: HMSO).

Department for Education and Employment and Department for Trade and Industry (2001) *Opportunity for All in a World of Change* (London: DTI). Available at http://www.dti.gov.uk/opportunityforall/pages/exec_sum.html#goal

Department for Education and Skills (2003b) *White Paper: 21st Century Skills, Realising Our Potential* (London: DfES). Available at http://www.dfes.gov.uk/skillsstrategy/subPage.cfm?action=whitePaper.default.

Department for Innovation Universities and Skills (2007) *World Class Skills: Implementing the Leitch Review of Skills in England*. Cm7181 (Norwich: HMSO).

Department for Trade and Industry (2002) *Social Enterprise: A Strategy for Success* (London: Department of Trade and Industry).

Department for Work and Pensions (2006) *A New Deal for Welfare: Empowering People to Work* (London: The Stationery Office).

Department for Work and Pensions (2007a) *In Work, Better Off: Next Steps to Full Employment*. Cm7130 (London: The Stationery Office).

Department for Work and Pensions (2007b) *Working for Children*. Cm7067 (London: The Stationery Office).

Dewson, S. (2005) *Evaluation of the Working Neighbourhood Pilot: Year One*. DWP Research Report 297 (London: Department for Work and Pensions). Available at http://www.dwp.gov.uk/asd/asd5/rports2005-2006/rrep297.pdf

Dickens, R., Gregg, P. & Wadsworth, J. (2000) New Labour and the labour market, *Oxford Review of Economic Policy*, 16(1), pp. 95–113.

Egan Review (2004) *Skills for Sustainable Communities* (London: Department for Communities and Local Government).

European Commission (2007) *Towards Common Principles of Flexicurity: More and Better Jobs Through Flexibility and Security* (Luxembourg: Office for Official Publications of the European Communities).

Finn, D. (2003) The employment first welfare state: Lessons from the New Deal for Young People, *Social Policy and Administration*, 37(7), pp. 708–725.

Freud, D. (2007) *Reducing Dependency, Increasing Opportunity: Options for the Future of Welfare to Work: An Independent Report to the Department for Work and Pensions* (Leeds: DWP).

Geddes, M. & Newman, I. (1999) Evolution and conflict in local economic development, *Local Economy*, 14(1), pp. 12–27.

Griffiths, R., Durkin, S., & Mitchell, A. (2006) Evaluation of the Single Provider Employment Zone Extension, Department for Work and Pensions Research Report 312 (London: DWP). Available at: http://www.dwp.gov.uk/asd/asd5/rports2005-2006/rrep312.pdf

Haahr, J. H. & Andersen, T. (2006) *Flexicurity in a Context of Restructuring. Contribution to the Mutual Learning Programme of the European Employment Strategy*. Discussion Paper (Aarhus: Danish Technological Institute).

Hallgarten, J. & Watling, R. (2001) Buying power: The role of the private sector in Education Action Zones, *School Leadership and Management*, 21(1), pp. 143–157.

Harker, L. (2006) *Delivering on Child Poverty: What Would it Take? A Report to the Department for Work and Pensions* (London: The Stationery Office).

Hirst, A., Tarling, R., Lefaucheux, M., Short, C., Rinne, S., McGregor, A., Glass, A., Evans, M. & Simm, C. (2006) *Evaluation of multiple provider employment zones*, Department for Work and Pensions Research Report 310 (London: DWP) http://www.dwp.gov.uk/asd/asd5/rports2005-2006/rrep310.pdf

HM Treasury (1999) *The Modernisation of Britain's Tax and Benefit System No.* 4: *Tackling Poverty and Extending Opportunity*. March (London: HM Treasury). Available at http://www.hm-treasury.gov.uk/media//B04CC/3.pdf

HM Treasury (2002) *The Modernisation of Britain's Tax and Benefit System No.* 10: *The Child and Working Tax Credits* (London: HM Treasury). Available at http://www.hm-treasury.gov.uk/media//EE15F/new_tax_credits.pdf

HM Treasury (2006) *A Strong and Strengthening Economy: Investing in Britain's Future*. HC968I (London: The Stationery Office).

Hooghe, L. & Marks, G. (2001a) *Multi-level Governance and European Integration* (Boulder: Rowman & Littlefield).

Hooghe, L. & Marks, G. (2001b) Types of multi-level governance, *European Integration Online Papers*, 5(1). Available at http://eiop.or.at/eiop/texte/2001-011.htm

Jessop, B. (2007) New Labour or the normalisation of neo-liberalism?, *British Politics*, 2(2), pp. 282–288.

Jones, A. & Ennis, N. (2007) Bringing the environment into economic development, *Local Economy*, 22(1), pp. 1–5.

Labour Party (1997) *New Labour because Britain Deserves Better: 1997 General Election Manifesto* (London: Labour Party).

Leitch (2006) *Prosperity for All in the Global Economy – World Class Skills, Final Report* (London: HMSO).

Low Pay Commission (1998) *The National Minimum Wage: The First Report of the Low Pay Commission* (London: Low Pay Commission).

Newman, J. (2005) *Remaking Governance: Peoples, Politics and the Public Sphere* (London: Policy Press).

Nunn, A. (2006) What next for New Labour after Blair?, *State of Nature*, (Nov./Dec.).

Nunn, A. (2007) Competitiveness and the New Labour project, *Papers in the Politics of Global Competitiveness*, 8(Sept.), pp. 1–30.

Office of Public Sector Reform (2002) *Public Service Reform: Principles into Practice* (London: Cabinet Office).

Piore, M. & Sabel, C. (1984) *The Second Industrial Divide: Possibilities for Prosperity* (New York: Basic Books).

Policy Research Institute (2006) *Phase 2 Evaluation of Multiple Provider Employment Zones: Qualitative Study* (London: Department for Work and Pensions). Available at http://www.dwp.gov.uk/asd/asd5/rports2005-2006/rrep399.pdf

Rhodes, R. (1996) The new governance: Governing without government, *Political Studies*, XLIV, pp. 652–667.

Rhodes, R. (1997) *Understanding Governance: Policy Networks, Governance, Reflexivity and Accountability* (Milton Keynes: Open University Press).

Sector Skills Development Agency (2003a) *Raising Performance Through Skills, Strategic Plan 2003-6* (Nottingham: Department for Education and Skills). Available at http://www.ssda.org.uk/pdfs/raise-full.pdf

Sector Skills Development Agency (2003) *The Skills and Productivity Challenge: A Summary of the Evidence Base for the SSDA's Strategic Plan* 2003–6 (Nottingham: Department for Education and Skills). Available at http://www.ssda.org.uk/pdfs/strat-evidence.pdf

Stern, N. (2006) *The Stern Review: The Economics of Climate Change* (Cambridge: Cambridge University Press).

Waddell, G. & Burton, A. K. 2006. *Is work good for your health and well being?* (London: The Stationery Office).

Wilthagen, T. (2007) *Flexicurity Practices* (Brussels: European Commission).

FEATURES

The Soft Spaces of Local Economic Development

GRAHAM HAUGHTON & PHIL ALLMENDINGER

ABSTRACT This article examines soft spaces, soft outcomes and soft infrastructure, trying to make some connections between them. We argue that soft spaces of governance constitute one of the most important but little understood components of contemporary sub-national economic development policy.

New Approaches to Local Economic Development

This article outlines some of the ways in which local economic development's traditional concerns with hard projects with hard outcomes are being not so much superseded as complemented by softer approaches to foster 'soft' outcomes, not least in building networks, partnerships and institutional capacity. The contemporary governance of local economic development, we want to argue, is being driven by three broad factors.

First, the need to work within and between formal institutional arrangements and statutory plans and strategies. Such formal or hard arrangements currently exist at scales that do not always map readily onto networks, policy sectors or appropriately scaled analytical understandings of particular issues or sites. Second, the rise of fragmentary, impermanent governance and funding structures. Institutional survival increasingly requires attention to building alliances that can successfully compete for new economic opportunities, government funding and the right to run politically in-favour governance structures. Third, the realisation that successful places and economies are as much a product of the existence and 'thickness' of public services and facilities (health, welfare, childcare etc) as hard infrastructure, such as roads and utilities. These driving forces towards a concern with the necessity for matching hard growth with soft outcomes reflect a particular Anglo-European 'new regionalist' philosophy about the importance of building institutional and regional capacity, notably through the creation of various networks, alliances and partnerships.

The argument here is most certainly not that the emergent systems of governance are somehow 'soft'. Far from it. Competing for institutional survival and for successes in providing the outputs required by funding providers requires highly competitive attitudes and actions. Rather, we want to argue for the importance to effective governance of engaging with three forms of softness – soft outcomes, soft spaces and soft infrastructure – which are characteristic if not emblematic of how governance is changing. We also want to highlight how governance structures and boundaries themselves are blurring and replacing the traditional notions of hard administrative boundaries with fuzziness.

Governance, Multilevel Governance and Relational Geographies

Governance has risen up the agenda as a political consensus appears to have developed that the role of government is no longer to 'do' economic development largely by direct intervention in the market. Rather it has become part of the role of government to encourage a multiplicity of sub-national governance structures through which visions, strategies, funding and delivery responsibilities can be agreed, shared and, hopefully, carried out. For some the result is confusion, little different to the days of the patchwork quilt of idiosyncrasy in urban regeneration funding (Audit Commission, 1989, 1999).

But actually it is very different. The current version of the patchwork approach is not driven by the same forces as earlier, cruder forms of neoliberalism. Instead, it represents a more pragmatic acceptance that the role of the state during the current period of neoliberal policy domination has changed, with less overt intervention in favour of a more steering mode of governance, linked to a rhetorical commitment to sustainable development, devolution, community-led responses and greater individual choice in accessing government services. The result is further differentiated from the 1980s through a very different tone, style and intent. In the new system of fast policy, continuous audit and market simulation, the state acts as partner, broker, funder and regulator, providing strategic selectivity over who is empowered and with this a strategic steer, all in an effort to promote national economic growth by seeking selectively to kickstart particular forms of development (see also Jessop, 2000).

When the programmes and institutions of the new governance systems are deemed to be failing by whatever criteria, change can quickly be ushered in. In arguing for change the case is frequently put for policies being constructed at alternative spatial scales, be it regional, sub-regional or neighbourhood, breaking away from past institutional forms that may be portrayed as not reflecting the real geographies of needs or opportunities, or being ossified into dysfunctional relationships. This rescaling of policy becomes justified discursively through creating a closer link to some imagined new sense of local 'community' or regional sensibility.

Such governance changes then always represent a way of breaking away from the past and ushering in new institutional forms to deliver highly selective agendas for change. Multilevel governance is important in this as it echoes the growing practice of constituting multiple levels of policy intervention reflecting new scalar relationships, which are neither hierarchical nor unilinear in shaping how power and knowledge flows across the new institutional assemblages. What is interesting for us is that this is not about creating a single new privileged scale of policy, but reworking policy across all scales, some long established, some new.

Recent work on relational geographies (Amin, 2002; Massey, 2005) usefully captures the stretched nature of associational networks that make formal government boundaries ever less relevant to many real world experiences and practices. In part it represents a critique of 'bounded' studies of particular areas, which can conceal as much as they reveal. Relational approaches emphasise the multiplicity of different networks and geographies that most of us actually operate within and across. For some of these networks proximity might be an important issue, whilst others might stretch globally, typically in patchy, uneven, rather messy ways.

So we may have important networks focused mainly around neighbouring areas and others that link us with, let us say Sydney, Santiago and Sydenham. What is important then is the way in which different types of relationship are constructed and conducted across variable geographies, involving highly varied institutional assemblages, connecting across space and time in ways that defy simplistic analysis that assumes that policy impacts work in some direct, unilinear fashion.

Metagovernance: The Hard Edge of the Soft State?

Governance, multilevel governance and metagovernance are now part of the rubric of local economic development. The political economy of multilevel governance has been central to a particularly productive academic debate concerning the changing role of the nation state under neoliberalism, involving debates about the variable fortunes and roles of political agendas on regionalism, the nation state, European expansion and globalisation. It is helpful to think of these various rescaling activities not so much as a single 'event' or even 'trend', such as the loss of nation state powers, but as a more complex and interrelated set of multiscalar changes.

For instance the 'hollowing out of the nation state' idea rests on the notion of states 'lending' powers selectively vertically up and down to other scales of governance, and horizontally, to new actors, such as business and community interests. But this reworking and rescaling of responsibilities across the tiers of governance does not imply a loss of power to the nation state, which retains control through its strategic selectivity in who it lends powers to, on what terms, and how it chooses to redraw and redefine its distribution of powers over time. The nation state still governs, but it does this increasingly at arms' length through guiding the everchanging 'rules of the game' (Jessop, 2000). More than this, it guides the process of 'filling-in' the hollowed out state, creating new institutional assemblages at sub-national levels (Goodwin *et al.*, 2005).

This is what is meant by metagovernance, or the steering of governance. For all the talk of bringing in local knowledge and resources, most partnerships are closely choreographed in the moves they can make by some fairly prescriptive rules, though it must be stressed that these are not simply externally imposed by the state in some predetermined way to a particular agenda. Rather the emerging rules of the game are struggled over by different societal forces at and across various scales. For instance, the very process of local and regional partnership making creates its own pressures for conformity, if not unity, in agreeing which behaviours and visions are deemed acceptable to the majority of partners (see e.g. Jessop, 2000, 2004, and Goodwin *et al.*, 2005).

It is in this context of multilevel governance and emergent agendas steered through systems of metagovernance that we are seeing a set of regional and city-regional experiments to find a new spatioinstitutional fix for the economic problems of areas, characterised by fluidity, rapidity and ruthlessness in how new solutions are arrived at, evaluated, extended, altered or discarded. So when we see proposals for city-regional powers, for instance, we need to see these as a reworking of the relations between regions, city-regions, local government and neighbourhoods. Powerful forces will align behind or against such proposals, working out what institutional forms best suit their needs.

In arguing their case they will typically bring in expert consultancy and academic expertise, carefully selecting those facts that best serve them, then using these strategically in presentations to government ministers, advisors, civil servants and the media. Whether originating from government or outside, then, new institutional forms invariably reflect dominant interests and are based on selective understandings of what constitute past failure and how best to judge future success.

Measuring Success through Hard Outputs and 'Soft' Outcomes

One of the implications of recent changes in governance for our understanding of local economic development is that increasingly we need to examine how the sector works alongside others in bringing about successful place making. In part this is reflected in the modernising government agenda of the past ten years, with its emphasis on joined-up policy in pursuit of a more holistic vision for improving local quality of life. This is a fairly marked shift from how traditional work in, and analysis of, local economic development and area regeneration was constructed.

Evaluation research has long been a cornerstone of both professional practice and academic endeavour, with recent years adding specific challenges. First, the need to situate local economic development within a broader policy mandate of improving quality of life brings with it a need for widening the scope of evaluation beyond narrow economic indicators. Second, there has been a concern to move beyond narrow project outputs, and their additive net outputs, towards broader based outcomes, taking a longer term, broader and more integrated perspective on the nature of change. Third, taking a lead from the policy interest in the social economy and academic interest in alternative evaluation tools such as social audit, there has been a shift towards assessing some of the so-called 'soft' outcomes of policy interventions, such as community capacity building, political reengagement, social capital, feelings of safety and confidence in an area (Hart & Haughton, 2007). These softer outcomes might then be measured through resident and 'customer' surveys, or proxy measures such as residential turnover, property rentals, or waiting lists for rented housing in an area.

With research effort often dictated by the availability of government funding for evaluation studies, the tendency in the past was to develop research strategies which would set out to see if Policy X, delivered by Institution Y, brought about a particular form of desired change in Area Z. There was perhaps little wrong with this in traditional evaluation terms when looking at traditional 'hard' local economic development practices. But everything is wrong with it when we begin to acknowledge that changed practices are situated in tangled webs of governance involving feedbacks that work across a variety of geographies, sectoral boundaries and timescales, and not through readily measured direct and indirect impacts. When variable institutional and local contexts, negative and positive synergistic effects, path dependency and institutional learning are factored in, the naivety of past forms of evaluation quickly become evident. Understanding this complexity does not give rapid, easily digested policy lessons, which in an era of evidence-based policy is problematic.

In essence we have become more sophisticated in our approach to evaluation but our understanding of the indeterminacies involved in linking policies with specific outcomes still fails to inform policy sufficiently. Producing good quality evaluation and policy research that goes beyond saying things are complex and multifaceted remains one of the challenges for local economic development if it is to prove its future worth.[1]

[1] These issues have been grappled with in two recent reports, one on policy outcomes in areas of deprivation, which found little hard evidence to back up recent policy to bolster enterprise in these areas (CCRS and MTL Consultants, 2005), and one on social enterprise impacts (Hart & Haughton, 2007).

Hard and Soft Spaces of Governance

One of the changes that most interests us has been the emergence of what we refer to as the 'soft' institutional spaces of governance (Allmendinger & Haughton, forthcoming; Haughton & Allmendinger, 2007b). Starting out by looking at spatial planning practices and their claimed centrality as a device for adding the essential 'spatial' dimension to more joined-up or integrated policy making, it emerged that much of the real work of 'strategic planning' was taking place outside the formal and/or statutory mechanisms of planning. Formal planning mechanisms with their legal responsibilities are primarily rooted in local and (to a lesser extent) regional government.

These are the hard spaces of governance activity, involving statutory responsibilities, linked to legal obligations including democratic engagement and consultation, all of which take time, and come with a particular set of public and professional expectations around their choreography. This is fine and necessary – but for many politicians and their advisors, it also looks to be slow, bureaucratic and rigid. There is also a mismatch between the spatial scales at which such planning is undertaken and the more amorphous, fluid and functional requirements of development and cross-sectoral working.

And this is where the emergent alternative administrative geographies, or the soft spaces of governance, have a role to play, providing a series of alternative institutional spaces in which to imagine possibilities for future place making. In a sense, we've had them for some years now – the Urban Development Corporations of old, followed by inner city Task Forces, City Challenge areas. More recently though we have seen a trend towards commissioning area 'Masterplans', plus all those pilots, prototypes and other brave new world experiments such as Employment Zones and New Deal for Communities. These new institutional forms and spaces are invariably mandated to 'break free' of past rigidities, to introduce innovative thinking and new practices that can be learned from and adopted elsewhere.

We want to argue three things here in relation to soft spaces. First, this is a deliberate attempt to insert new opportunities for creative thinking, particularly in areas where public engagement and cross-sectoral consultation has seen entrenched oppositional forces either slowing down or freezing out most forms of new development. Second, that the 'hard' and 'soft' spaces of governance are mutually constitutive. One cannot work without the other. The aim is not to remove 'hard' institutional spaces with new 'softer' ones, rather to create complementary and potentially competing opportunities for development activities to focus around, whether at some kind of 'sub' regional or 'sub' local government scale. Third, the soft spaces of governance are becoming more numerous and more important as part of the institutional landscape of regeneration.

Think of the Government's Sustainable Communities initiative for instance, creating four Growth Areas, only one of which approximates local government boundaries, and the numerous Housing Market Renewal

Pathfinder areas, none of which are coincident with local government areas. Thames Gateway is one of the Growth Areas. It is not coterminous with any other institutional actor. Covering three government regions and 16 local authorities and Local Strategic Partnerships it has within it a variety of other delivery forms including two new-style UDCs, the Olympic Delivery Agency, three sub-regional partnerships (Thames Gateway London, Thames Gateway South Essex and Thames Gateway Kent Partnership), one Urban Regeneration Company and six other local partnerships. On top of this are numerous local area Masterplans, in South East Thurrock and Southend for instance.

Alongside these new institutional geographies, or soft spaces operating at various scales, there are still the important 'hard' spaces of traditional governmental functions. So formal planning functions meantime operate at the level of the regions and local government. Local governments also provide local economic development functions, housing strategies, leisure strategies, cultural strategies, sustainable community strategies and more.

The Future of Governance: Soft, Hard and Fuzzy

The relationship between hard and soft spaces is one that the Government appears to be aware of and keen to develop. It is a truism that no institutional spatial-fix is ideal: there will always be a range of networks across and between administrations and organisations. In the past the scope and scale of institutional arrangements have been dealt with through 'hard' reorganisations of local and regional government. Local government reorganisations in the 1970s, 1990s and the creation of regional bodies in 2004 attempted to better reflect and balance the changed needs of governance. However, such reorganisations are extremely costly, contentious and tend to create as many problems as they resolve. A number of recent moves by Government point to the acceptance and formalisation of soft spaces in governance.

First, as has become clear to anyone involved in regional level economic development and planning, most Regional Economic Strategies and Regional Spatial Strategies are, in effect, amalgams of sub-regional plans. Sometimes introduced with fanfare and fuzzy boundaries as new ways of thinking and behaving, as in the initial announcements on the city-regions in the Northern Way, and the subregions in the Wales Spatial Plan, over time pragmatic considerations tend to lead to some reversion to working creatively with existing institutional geographies. But the new thinking around institutional geographies is emblematic of a discontent with previous approaches and a willingness to accept multiple regionalisms emerging. Functional areas for planning and economic development based around travel-to-work and housing market areas already exist beyond the administrative and plan making boundaries of many local authorities. Towns such as Reading and Torquay have very tight administrative boundaries. It makes sense, as the Government point out, to look to a town's hinterland for plan and strategy making. Sir Michael Lyons underlined this in his recent report, rejecting the call for another round of local government organisation. Instead, he argued there should be a 'stronger emphasis on the responsibility of authorities to develop effective and flexible coalitions which transcend boundaries, and to seek joint solutions to problems where those offer potential advantages' (2007, para. 70). Multi Area Agreements (MAAs) are just part of the array of tools that are being used to encourage greater collaboration across traditional local government boundaries.

Second, the Treasury-led Government consultation paper on Sub-National Economic Development and Regeneration (HM Treasury, 2007) has argued for the need to support subregions and city regions, allowing economic development matters to be dealt with at that scale. This could involve allowing local authorities to come to agreements to pool resources and strategy making across boundaries, giving such agreements both statutory backing and greater financial support.

Third, the Housing and Planning Delivery Grant will in future reward local authorities for working across boundaries to create functional planning areas. This will reinforce existing guidance to local authorities on functional planning and joint work already on housing and the guidance on economic development and employment in the form of draft Planning Policy Statement 4.

Of course formalising informal arrangements comes with its own dangers. Professionals will need to begin to think more strategically about what happens at the 'edge' of their areas of responsibility, the relationship to existing plans, strategies and democratic accountability begins to be questioned, and the legitimacy of more formal soft arrangements is open to question and challenge.

Soft and Hard Infrastructures in Support of Development

Finally here, we want to argue that greater attention needs to be given to organising effective forms of infrastructure provision and maintenance. At the moment, the sector is reasonably well versed in working at site level towards providing hard infrastructure such as site preparation, land reclamation, energy, water, drainage, flood protection and transport, but less practiced in terms of lobbying for soft infrastructure, or for dealing with the wider local, sub-regional and regional implications of cumulative demands being made on infrastructure. We are particularly concerned that growth is currently not being 'managed' in ways that reflect porous boundaries and long-term horizons. Instead short-term incrementalism in infrastructure provision remains the norm, where the external impacts of an area's development are ignored wherever possible in pursuit of rapid decisions, short-term political gains and higher private profits. The result will be potential chaos in some of the larger growth areas – and also in areas where infrastructure capacity is being reached.

Far from arguing that local economic development is on some path that moves away from achieving hard outcomes, we want to suggest that the sector will be increasingly required to reengage with those providing both the hard and the soft infrastructures that make localities 'liveable'. But it is soft infrastructure that economic developers and planners alike currently fail to deal with adequately, covering issues such as where best to locate and how to fund the provision of clinics, hospitals, hospices, day care for young and old, homes for the elderly, schools, universities, parks and other green spaces. In an ideal world, this would be part of the wider urban and rural renaissance policy impetus for development professionals to deal more productively in creating the conditions for producing well-designed neighbourhoods, melding high quality urban aesthetics, and clean, safe, usable public spaces that together create a strong and positive sense of place.

Bland no-place developments can detract from an area's long-term success, not add to it. When mobile investors and workers are deciding where to locate, it is precisely these quality of place issues that are increasingly influential. At the moment, however, the emphasis remains on producing rapid physical development, ideally a bit more 'sustainable' in some ways and less ugly, whilst social infrastructure issues still go begging (Haughton & Allmendinger, 2007a).

In recent years the tendency has been to get carried away by the attractions of 'cultural policies' for cities. This is fine, of course, but it is not enough, and it should not be allowed to become a diversion from getting the basics right, working with governance partners to ensure high quality infrastructure is provided in a timely fashion, in appropriate locations, and with a strong governance system to ensure financial and institutional durability. Ad hoc developments that make incremental demands on wider infrastructure without due regard to capacity and maintenance are no longer acceptable. Events such as the floods in Hull during 2007 reveal how poorly negotiated new development and upgraded but undercapacity (drainage) infrastructure is not sustainable development (Coulthard *et al.*, 2007) and can quickly undermine many years of place promotion and other forms of economic development activity.

Conclusions

We are perhaps used to thinking that traditional 'hard' economic development activities needs to be complemented by a greater understanding of the potential for community-based or 'soft' activities, measured through incorporating better measures for soft outcomes. We want to take this argument further.

First, we need to better understand the intersection of the soft and hard spaces of governance, not least who currently uses them, and how, and the specific implications for the future role of economic development. Recent research has highlighted how economic development, strongly linked to urban regeneration, is leading in the use of soft spaces as a means to affect change (Allmendinger & Haughton, forthcoming). The more flexible and fluid arenas for negotiation and the quicker, less regulatory-stymied atmosphere required by schemes that cross administrative boundaries are well suited to the pragmatisms of such approaches. Economic development increasingly acts as a broker between public sector-focused hard spaces and the demands of economic development and regeneration.

Second, successful economic development will rely as much upon place making as place promotion and the provision of sites and premises. How we go about evaluating such broader approaches is not well understood and currently rather hit and miss. In an era of clearly defined targets and measures such as GVA growth more subjective evaluations will be more time consuming and costly. Moreover, as the government seeks to rationalise the number of its targets in search of greater simplicity, it will be important to hold out for targets that reflect a wider rather than a narrower vision of local economic development.

Third, practitioners will need to revert to a more active engagement with ensuring adequate soft and hard infrastructure is put in place to support future development, not simply to gain efficiencies and economies in provision, but to ensure the sustainability of the quality of life of an area. More than this, economic development will need to promote well-designed commercial areas and residential neighbourhoods, and not just in 'prestige sites', aiming to create liveable communities where investors want to invest, workers want to work, and people want to live.

Finally, not all the emerging arrangements will work. Evaluations of in what circumstances and in what ways successful soft space economic development and planning adds value to existing approaches is required. The potential downsides, as highlighted in the Thames Gateway, include highly complex and time consuming arrangements that may be offputting to potential developers and firms.

Acknowledgements

This work was funded under ESRC grant number RES-000-23-0756. Many thanks to referees and Ines Newman for some constructive comments on our earlier draft.

References

Allmendinger, P. & Haughton, G. (forthcoming) Soft spaces, fuzzy boundaries and metagovernance: The new spatial planning in the Thames Gateway, *Environment and Planning A*.

Amin, A. (2002) Spatialities of globalisation, *Environment and Planning A*, 34(3), pp. 385–399.

Audit Commission (1989) *Urban Regeneration and Economic Development: The Local Government Dimension* (London: HMSO).

Audit Commission (1999) *A Life's Work: Local Authorities, Economic Development and Urban Regeneration* (Abingdon: Audit Commission).

CCRS and MTL Consultants (2006) *Policy Interactions and Outcomes in Deprived Areas*. BERR Report URN 05/1748. Available at http://www.berr.gov.uk/files/file38342.pdf

Coulthard, T., *et al.* (2007) *The June 2007 Floods in Hull. Final report of the Independent Review Body*. Available at http://www.coulthard.org.uk/downloads/floodsinhull3.pdf

Goodwin, M., Jones, M. & Jones, R. (2005) Devolution, constitutional change and economic development: understanding the shifting economic and political geographies of the British state, *Regional Studies*, 39, pp. 421–436.

Hart, T. & Haughton, G. (2007) *Assessing the Economic and Social Impacts of Social Enterprise: Feasibility Report* (Cabinet Office). Available at http://www.cabinetoffice.gov.uk/upload/assets/www.cabinetoffice.gov.uk/third_sector/assessing_impact_se_full.pdf

Haughton, G. & Allmendinger, P. (2007a) Growth and social infrastructure in spatial planning, *Town and Country Planning*, 76(Nov.), pp. 388–391.

Haughton, G. & Allmendinger, P. (2007b) 'Soft spaces' in planning, *Town and Country Planning*, 76(Sept.), pp. 306–308.

HM Treasury (2007) *Review of Sub-National Economic Development and Regeneration* (London: HMSO).

Jessop, B. (2000) The crisis of the national spatio-temporal fix and the ecological dominance of globalizing, *International Journal of Urban and Regional Research*, 24(2), pp. 323–360.

Jessop, B. (2004) Multi-level governance and multi-level metagovernance changes in the European Union as integral moments in the transformation and reorientation of contemporary statehood, in: I. Bache & M. Flinders (Eds) *Multi-Level Governance*, pp. 49–74 (Oxford: Oxford University Press).

Lyons, M. (2007) *The Lyon's Inquiry into Local Government. Executive Summary* (London: HMSO).

Massey, D. (2005) *For Space* (London: Sage).

FEATURES

A New Policy for Britain's Cities: Choices, Challenges, Contradictions

IVAN TUROK

ABSTRACT The general perception of cities has been transformed over the last decade. The purpose of the article is to consider the idea and reality of urban revitalisation and to examine whether the government's emerging spatial policy will help to strengthen and sustain the revival. Evidence shows that there has been a significant improvement in urban economic conditions in recent years, but the short-term outlook is less favourable. While the government has taken some useful steps along the road to a more effective policy for cities, there is further to go. There are also important dilemmas to be addressed that go beyond a simple spatial fix.

There has been a sea change in the way cities are perceived over the last decade. The last special issue of *Local Economy* in 1999 was dominated by problems of urban decline and difficulties in securing regeneration. Today cities are in vogue among consumers, tourists and investors, with a physical transformation underway in many city centres and waterfront locations. This is mirrored by a shift in government thinking – cities are now portrayed as vital economic and cultural assets and part of the solution to neighbourhood poverty and regional inequalities. But does Britain's urban renaissance go beyond glittering shopping malls, hotels and apartment blocks to provide a durable economic base fit for the twenty-first century? And will the government's emerging sub-national policy really help to strengthen and sustain the revival of former industrial areas?

The object of this article is to consider the changing economic fortunes of Britain's cities and to try and tease out the implications of current developments in sub-national (or 'spatial') policy, a broad term used to cover neighbourhoods, cities and regions. I examine whether the apparent improvements in urban conditions over the last decade have been meaningful. I also ask what difference government policy is likely to make to the prospects of achieving an enduring and broad-based revitalisation of major urban areas. This involves exploring some of the tensions emerging from the important 2007 review of sub-national economic development and regeneration (SNR), the expectations of which had been so high (HM Treasury, 2007b).

The article is organised as follows. The first three sections explain why there is a renewed sense of optimism about the position of cities from the perspective of government policy. The following two sections review the arguments and evidence surrounding the economic revival of cities. The final sections examine the scope for improving urban conditions, and the implications for local economic development policy, including some of the dilemmas faced.

The New Urban Agenda

For many years cities were perceived by UK governments to be victims of economic decline, sources of social breakdown and places of environmental decay. Deindustrialisation, worsening poverty and selective outmigration eroded the fabric of many urban communities and weakened civic institutions. Some commentators portrayed cities as obsolete legacies of an industrial era of high transport costs, local supply linkages and people living close to work. In a 'post-industrial' world of cheap travel and higher incomes, households and firms naturally preferred lower density locations with less congestion and greener environments (e.g. Pascal, 1987).

This antiurban ethos has been turned on its head in recent years. A new urban narrative has taken hold, with cities portrayed as centres of economic dynamism and places that can help to solve many contemporary challenges (HM Treasury, 2006, 2007b; Scottish Executive, 2006). For example, they nourish innovation and foster the productivity growth vital for an advanced economy to be 'smarter' by creating distinctive products and services that command premium prices. Cities are also supposed to contain the amenities, education institutions and career opportunities to help regions and nations attract the specialised skills and talent required to generate and exploit original knowledge and build the dynamic competitive advantage to sustain their success.

The new urban thinking is reflected in a barrage of recent government reports, white papers, legislation, ad hoc initiatives and institutional reforms, particularly in England. It has been lent added significance by the Treasury's recent commitment to the new agenda. For many years it seemed sceptical about the economic potential of old industrial cities and regions. Spending on regeneration and all aspects of spatial policy was regarded as essentially unproductive or 'zero-sum'. The official evaluation framework treated them as 'distributional', assuming that improvements in one area come at the expense of others through displacement or crowding out (see e.g. Department of Environment, Transport and the Regions–DETR, 1997; Office of the Deputy Prime Minister–ODPM, 2004). Urban and regional development could make no contribution to increased productive capacity, productivity or economic output, almost by definition.

This is beginning to change (Communities and Local Government–CLG, 2007; HM Treasury, 2006, 2007b), with greater recognition being given to various ways in which 'place', and therefore urban policy, can contribute to national prosperity, or undermine it if neglected.[1] For example, cities may promote growth by improving firms' access to information and specialised services, enabling learning and technological progress through knowledge spillovers, and ensuring better labour market matching between workers and employers. By improving the efficiency of the transport system, expanding the supply of land for housing and ensuring a more responsive education and training system that increases the size and skills of the workforce, urban policy can also facilitate growth by removing constraints or 'negative externalities', such as congestion and overheating.

An influential cross-departmental report published with the 2006 Budget was the first real Treasury endorsement of the economic case for backing cities. It had a bold subtitle 'the importance of cities to regional growth' and it argued in considerable detail and with much supporting evidence that:

> Cities matter because the productivity benefits they provide to knowledge-intensive businesses are important for regional and national prosperity... Cities provide an opportunity to narrow the economic gap between our regions and to tackle deprivation at the local and neighbourhood levels. (HM Treasury, 2006, p. i)

Is City Policy Replacing Neighbourhood Policy?

The second part of the above quote is also important in signalling two new roles envisaged for a policy towards cities – narrowing regional inequalities and reducing neighbourhood poverty. This suggests a shift in spatial policy and warrants closer consideration. It appears from the SNR and other policy statements that city-level policy is taking precedence over neighbourhood policy and possibly regional policy too. This raises a question about the relationship between policies at the three scales. Put bluntly, are they substitutes or complementary? Departmental fragmentation has meant three parallel agendas in the past and the government is still wrestling with the task of formulating an integrated spatial policy. It must be possible to conceive of neighbourhood programmes nested within city-wide strategies, which in turn would relate to broader regional

[1] It should be said that this is not yet properly incorporated into the Treasury's Green Book or other guidance on the evaluation of spatial policy, which continue to assume that the effects are largely distributional. This probably reflects continuing tensions within and between the Treasury and other government departments on this issue.

and national economic and spatial planning frameworks to ensure a genuine joined-up approach.

The SNR was not specific about what should happen to neighbourhood policy, beyond the need to further concentrate the funding in the poorest areas. It also suggested that: 'neighbourhood renewal is probably best managed at the local authority level' (HM Treasury, 2007b, p. 66). Two indications of a change in the status of neighbourhood policy are the decisions late in 2007 to wind up the Neighbourhood Renewal Unit and to end dedicated funding streams for 39 different neighbourhood programmes tackling issues such as antisocial behaviour, drugs and teenage pregnancy. They will be replaced with a single nonringfenced budget for local authorities to support local priorities, and with a steer to devote more emphasis to economic development. Coincidentally, a similar decision was announced in Scotland to devolve regeneration funding, along with some of the business support and regeneration functions of Scottish Enterprise, to local authorities. Local Social Inclusion Partnerships had been wound up a year or so before this.

Neighbourhood policy had been high profile ever since Tony Blair's bold aim to transform conditions in poor estates so that within a decade or two no one would be disadvantaged by where they live. One reason for ringfencing was that many councils find it difficult politically to skew mainstream resources towards particular areas, so its demise could deprive poor neighbourhoods in some cities of these extra funds. Well-resourced programmes such as New Deal for Communities had themselves created controversy from other poor areas nearby that felt they were missing out (Home Office, 2001; Turok *et al.*, 2006), so some politicians may not be sorry to see them go. More importantly, there were concerns within the policy community that area-based initiatives were too fragmented and unfocused, with insufficient understanding of why the problems had arisen or how they might be resolved (Prime Minister's Strategy Unit–PMSU, 2005). At worst they were palliatives chasing the symptoms of poverty around the local partnership, rather than tackling the root causes by getting people jobs, improving their livelihoods and stabilising chaotic lifestyles. Worklessness seemed to underpin many problems of debt, stress, ill-health, addictions, family breakdown, children's behaviour and educational underachievement (Sanderson, 2006; Webster, 2006).

Doubts had also surfaced about the effectiveness of a bottom-up neighbourhood approach in the face of widening social inequalities and underlying economic weaknesses (Buck *et al.*, 2005; Lawless, 2006; Lupton, 2003; Parkinson *et al.*, 2006; Turok & Robson, 2007). Isolated area initiatives seemed to be overwhelmed by powerful forces at wider spatial scales transmitted through the local labour and housing markets. Concentrations of unemployment and poverty reflected a combination of insufficient jobs and residential sorting of low-skilled groups into the worst housing. The SNR echoed the view that a broader approach was needed: 'The success of neighbourhood renewal will depend on economic progress at wider spatial levels' (HM Treasury, 2007b, p. 15). One of the issues arising is whether growth will be promoted at too broad a scale (e.g. the city-region) to ensure that the poorest places benefit (Turok & Robson, 2007). Another is the extent to which linkage mechanisms will also be introduced to secure workless groups a fair share of the opportunities, including personalised support to increase skills and motivation, overcome various health and debt problems, and provide affordable childcare and supplementary early years provision (Turok, 2007a)?

Is City Policy Displacing Regional Policy?

Meanwhile regional policy has been recast over the last decade from a focus on economic modernisation through inward investment using government incentives for lagging regions. The new approach involves stimulating indigenous growth through development agencies in every region (Fothergill, 2005). Their function is to support the expansion of new and existing enterprises by improving workforce skills, management capabilities and infrastructure. Innovation is another recurring theme, typified by efforts to develop nascent industries, such as biotechnology or new materials, by translating university research in science and technology into commercial products. The government said it would build up regional institutional capacity by steadily decentralising powers and responsibilities. However, the failure of the 2004 North East referendum to endorse an elected regional assembly was a major setback and raised concerns about the accountability of the new organisations.

One of the attractions of the emerging 'city-regions' agenda is the prospect of filling the lacuna left by the stalled regional devolution project (Gonzalez *et al.*, 2006). The city-region idea is sufficiently flexible to cover many different kinds of places (Parr, 2005). It appeals to the interests of cities as well as surrounding towns and rural areas, including the Core Cities pressure group of the eight largest cities in England outside London. The new cities agenda fits in well with the approach to regional policy in focusing on indigenous development and innovation, so it could become the new focus of attention without a radical rethink. Furthermore, it offers an advantage over policies based on the standard regions: the possibility of capturing the economic benefits of agglomeration, including through more efficient planning of local housing markets and transport systems.

Part of the city-region appeal is that it encompasses functional housing and labour markets and resulting transport movements better than neighbourhoods or council areas, which are too small to cover many of the interactions. It is all too apparent that if a city-region isn't functioning well because of congestion or bottlenecks in housing supply then economic growth is likely to be held back. Treasury recognition of the inflationary effects of housing shortfalls in London and the South-East, and the sheer problems of affordability for first-time buyers, has resulted in highly ambitious (and expensive) plans to develop the Thames Gateway and other 'Growth Areas' (Eddington, 2006; ODPM, 2003, 2005). They are among the largest developments Britain has seen for decades.

The SNR recognises the importance of city-regions as engines of growth and a sensible level for planning housing and labour market interventions in many parts of the country: 'One of the key conclusions of this analysis is that there would be benefits in greater working at sub-regional level' (HM Treasury, 2007b, p. 67). However, its proposals to strengthen city-region decision making are modest and do nothing to streamline the organisational clutter. The big idea is voluntary Multi-Area Agreements reached between core city authorities, surrounding areas and other relevant bodies on shared priorities for economic development and housing. Some funding will be made available for up to three years to incentivise cooperation. These are seen as temporary arrangements, although the possibility of permanent organisations is mooted. The SNR also mentions proposals in the current Local Transport Bill for strengthening public transport bodies covering the former met counties and some new powers for local authorities to improve bus services and tackle traffic congestion.

Government reports and white papers emphasise repeatedly that differences between places really matter and that decentralised institutions are more sensitive to local needs and circumstances. Local knowledge means they are better placed to identify latent assets and to exploit opportunities than central government, which is too remote and bureaucratic (Department of Communities and Local Government–DCLG, 2006; HM Treasury, 2007b; OECD, 2006; Parkinson *et al.*, 2006). Consequently, decentralisation to local organisations should produce more responsive and successful policies.

In practice the level of devolution to date has been limited and 'many councils would admit to being disappointed by the speed of progress so far' (Centre for Cities, 2007, p. 1). The SNR indicates a desire to strengthen the role of local authorities in economic development by giving them more responsibility for 14- to 19-year-olds' education and training. It also states an intention to give them new scrutiny powers over RDAs and regional transport bodies, but merely to consult on new local authority powers and incentives to encourage growth. The lack of progress on new funding streams or flexibility to use existing income sources more creatively to fund capital projects is particularly disappointing. The Local Authority Business Growth Initiative has run into serious difficulties and the supplementary business rate proposals have been capped at a low level, so will yield few new resources in most places.

The Agglomeration Argument for Cities

The idea that cities make a disproportionate contribution to economic growth needs close scrutiny. The basic proposition is that geographical concentration (agglomeration) offers advantages of scale and dynamic competitiveness in an advanced economy. This may apply most to high order services and functions where intellectual resources (human intelligence, knowledge, skills etc) are more important than physical resources and more sensitive to distance decay. The SNR endorses this view, although if towns are included it is unclear what is left out: 'The growth of the knowledge economy, and services in particular, means that towns and cities are increasingly places of wealth creation' (HM Treasury, 2007b, p. 19).

It is difficult to disentangle and quantify the effects of agglomeration because of their complexity. In general, the bigger the city the better access firms may have to a deep labour pool, large customer base, choice of shared services and suppliers, and good external connections (Duranton & Puga, 2004; Turok, 2004). These benefits are offset by more congestion and higher labour and property costs, which would otherwise cause dispersal. In a context of changing markets and technologies there is a premium on flexibility, especially as companies are leaner and more reliant on buying-in goods and services rather than in-house production. Big cities enable firms to 'mix and match' their inputs and alter their workforce more easily in response to changing business needs (Buck *et al.*, 2005). This lowers costs, raises productivity and improves resilience.

Knowledge-intensive firms may also benefit from superior flows of ideas and information, resulting in more learning and innovation. This enables high cost economies to differentiate themselves from competitors by continually developing more valuable products, processes and services. Proximity facilitates face-to-face contact, high-level communication and sharing of complex ideas (Storper & Manville, 2006). Firms can compare, compete and cooperate, engendering a self-reinforcing dynamic that spurs progress, attracts mobile capital and talent, and generates growth from within. The most successful cities are sometimes said to operate as *knowledge hubs*, gateways or spikes in a more interconnected global system of information, trade and financial flows (Castells, 2000; European Commission, 2007; Hall & Pain, 2006). Advanced producer services are often portrayed as the key drivers of these cities, including banking and insurance, legal and accountancy services, advertising and design, consultancy, information technology and research. Nascent and creative industries, such as digital media, music and publishing, could also be included.

There is growing evidence from econometric studies that cities offer measurable advantages, both for businesses and workers (Duranton & Puga, 2004; Fingleton, 2003). A summary of the international research concluded that doubling city size increases productivity somewhere in the range from 3% to 8% (Rosenthal & Strange, 2004). A recent UK study measured this at 3.5% (Rice *et al.*, 2006). The advantages of proximity also diminished quickly with distance from the city: they were four times stronger 30 minutes driving-time away than 60 minutes away. This means that transport improvements to reduce travel times can have valuable productivity benefits if focused in and around major cities. Eddington

(2006) concluded that this should be the top priority for transport investment (see also, Marshall & Webber, 2007). Another UK study for the Department of Transport found even larger productivity gains varying between 8% for manufacturing and 13% for services (Graham, 2006). The biggest benefits were for financial services and professional services such as consultancy. This chimes with recent qualitative research on high order business services that found tendencies towards concentration outweighed dispersal across eight leading European city-regions (Hall & Pain, 2006).

Simple evidence on productivity, innovation and earnings across the UK seems to confirm the effects of agglomeration, with some qualifications. Thus, a city's industrial and occupational structure may override its size. Regional location is also important. For example, Edinburgh and York rank highly on these indicators despite their modest size (because of the strong presence of high value financial services and professional and managerial occupations), whereas larger cities like Liverpool, Glasgow, Newcastle and Sheffield do not (Centre for Cities, 2007; Jones, Williams, Lee, *et al.*, 2006). London is ranked higher than all other parts of the UK, effectively in a league of its own, although this is also far from just a function of its size (European Commission, 2007; Parkinson *et al.*, 2006; Rice *et al.*, 2006). Cities in the 'second division' are mostly in the South and East, including Cambridge, Oxford, Reading, Bristol, Southampton, Bournemouth and Derby. Studies of the geography of knowledge-intensive, creative and high-tech industries and occupations have found that London tends to dominate (Buck *et al.*, 2005; Department of Trade and Industry–DTI, 2001). It comes closest to the idea of a knowledge hub, although this is not the full story behind its recent success.

It is no coincidence that London has received increasing government support in recent years, including a special ministerial task force, major infrastructure projects for the 2012 Olympics, Thameslink, Crossrail, St Pancras and the Millennium Dome. The Greater London Authority under Ken Livingstone has also been granted wide-ranging new powers covering housing policy, planning, adult skills, health, water regulation, waste and culture in order to improve strategic decision making, prompting calls for the leaders of other cities to be given the same strategic capabilities (Centre for Cities, 2007). The idea of a supplementary business rate announced late in 2007 will be of most benefit to London and seems to be aimed at allowing additional fundraising for Crossrail. The government is committed to 'ensuring London sustains its success as the UK's only global city' (HM Treasury, 2007b, p. 91).

One of the big questions for spatial policy surrounds the economic relationships between London and cities in the North. This is a serious omission in the SNR and related documents, presumably because the government's approach to spatial policy plays down interregional issues in favour of intraregional and local concerns. The OECD recently criticised the strategies of Northern cities and regions for neglecting their actual and potential linkages with London (OECD, 2006). London's prosperity is fuelled partly by drawing in resources from other UK regions, including highly skilled and talented workers. But London's growth also supports jobs elsewhere by dispersing lower value activities (such as call centres) and funding higher public spending through taxes raised in London. The balance between these processes is very unclear and warrants further research. There is some evidence that the benefits of London's prosperity have been concentrated in the rest of the South-East (Hall & Pain, 2006; Lucci & Seex, 2007).

The SNR suggests that London's relative economic strengths mean that disparities with other UK regions are likely to widen in the years ahead. It is also probable that increased public investment in major infrastructure in the South-East, coupled with a large expansion of house-building, will weaken growth in the North by (1) reducing the pressures on employers (public as well as private) to relocate some of their activities and (2) accommodating a higher level of migration from North to South. Hence agglomeration is a double-edged argument for Northern cities. It does not automatically imply that they will prosper in a UK context, or that they can play a role in reducing regional disparities. One of the outcomes of the new spatial policy may be to justify a shift in public investment towards the South-East aimed at removing growth constraints and promoting knowledge-based industries in the interests of UK plc.

Diverse Development Paths for Cities

Outside London, the evidence suggests there has been an economic revival too, but it is quite uneven and more apparent in employment growth than productivity or innovation (HM Treasury, 2007b). The broad conclusion of the State of English Cities was that cities have turned around after several decades of decline, but they have not narrowed the prosperity gap with the rest of the country (Parkinson *et al.*, 2006; Turok *et al.*, 2006). City success was a less a function of size than its industrial and occupational structure, workforce skills, land supply, connectivity, amenities and strategic capacity of local institutions.

Figures 1 and 2 offer some original evidence to compare changes in employment for Britain's 20 largest cities between 1981–1996 and 1996–2005. The former is taken from a study that found a widening jobs gap between cities and other parts of the country, caused by deindustrialisation and deconcentration (Turok & Edge, 1999). In Figure 2 the index of change has been rebased to 1996 to help compare the two periods. It shows a striking improvement – absolute and relative – in the conurbations (Greater Manchester, Merseyside, West Midlands, South Yorkshire, West Yorkshire, Tyneside and Greater Glasgow). The 12 free-standing cities, including Coventry, Leicester, Nottingham, Hull and Plymouth, also improved, but not as much. Overall, this supports the idea that cities have generally 'picked-up', but not caught up with other places (see also, Centre for Cities, 2007; Webster, 2006). Deindustrialisation has

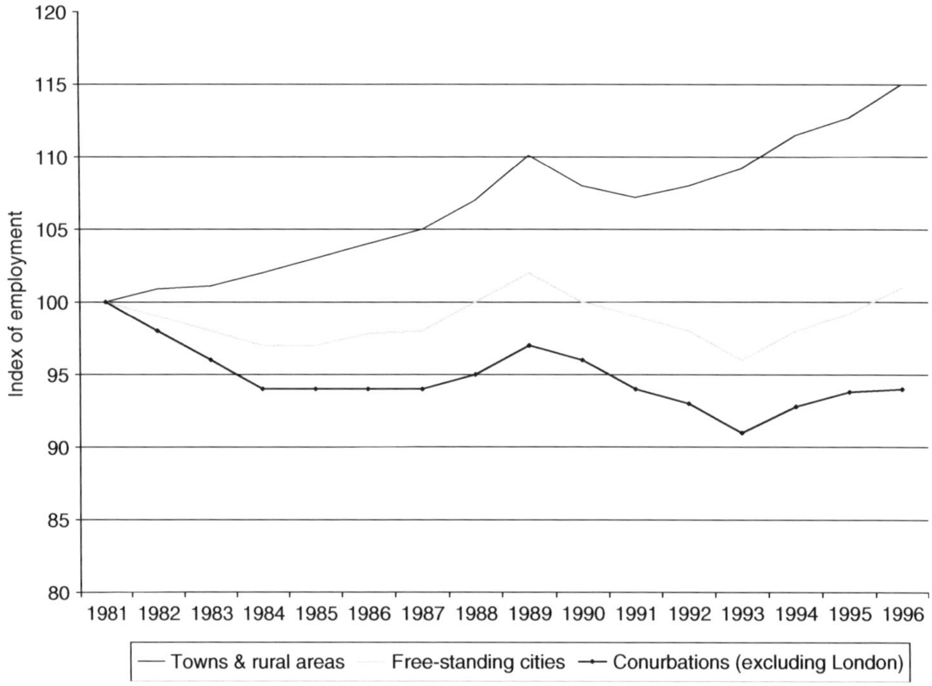

Figure 1. Total employment change by type of area (1981–1996) (1981 = 100). Source: Office for National Statistics (Annual Business Inquiry) via NOMIS

become less important with manufacturing jobs a smaller element of total employment, and the net urban–rural dispersal of employment generally seems to have declined, perhaps because of the stronger forces of concentration.

From the available evidence it also appears that the composition of growth has varied. The recovery of many cities seems to have had less to do with knowledge-intensive functions and more to do with 'extensive', job-rich forms of growth (European Commission, 2007; Jones, Williams, Coats, *et al.*, 2006; Turok & Mykhnenko, 2008). In an effort to capture this, Figure 3 portrays three distinctive sources of growth apparent over the last decade. It is broad-brush and seeks to reflect both industry and occupation dimensions. There is some indication of the source of demand, although it omits the contribution of higher public spending in sectors such as health and education. For the sake of simplicity it also omits the role of niche manufacturing and other specialisations.

Cities do not seem to have experienced one form exclusively, but elements of all three in different combinations. It is important for policy makers to understand the determinants of each better, including their limits and potential. An appropriate goal may be to find ways of upgrading a city's full range of assets over time to move beyond the relatively low skill, low productivity, low income status quo in order to generate higher 'quality'

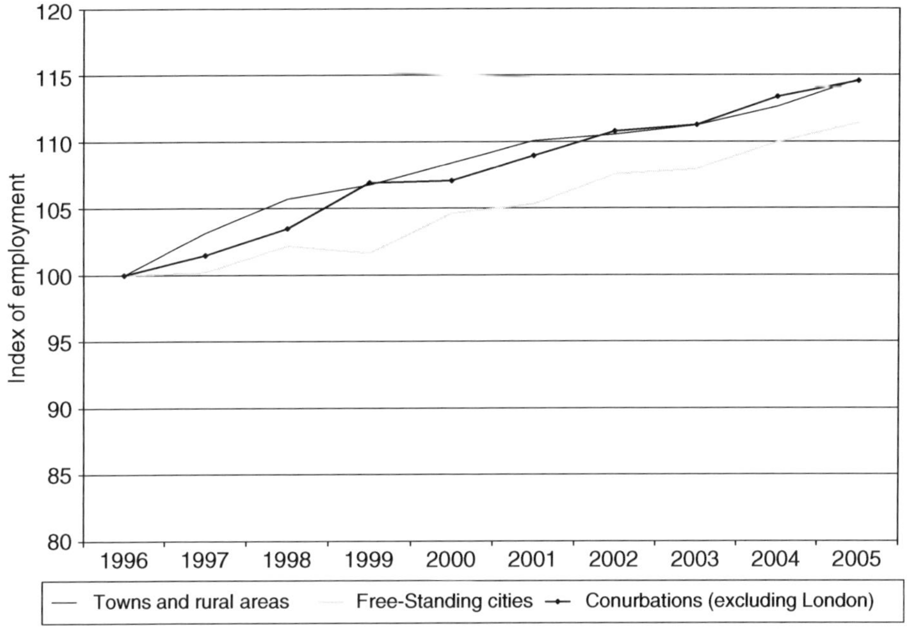

Figure 2. Total employment change by type of area (1996–2005) (1996 = 100). Source: Office for National Statistics (Annual Business Inquiry) via NOMIS

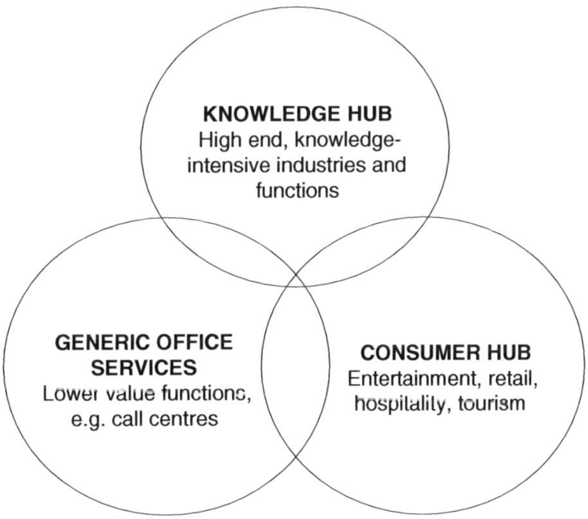

Figure 3. Different sources of city growth.

growth without excluding sections of the population. A narrowly defined *knowledge hub* (or 'Ideopolis' – Jones, Williams, Lee, *et al.*, 2006) should not be the only vision of a contemporary urban economy, especially if it unrealistic for some cities or too exclusive for others.

Generic office-based services are less easy to define than knowledge-intensive services. They cover a wide range of activities that may be less specialised or more standardised in nature, and therefore generate lower levels of value added per worker. Examples include call centres, data processing, IT support, customer services and a range of other administrative functions that are often cost-sensitive, outsourced and known as 'shared services'. They rely less on innovation and specialised graduate skills and more on the ready availability of modestly priced premises and white-collar labour. A responsive property market and ready supply of labour enables firms to adjust the scale of their operations more quickly to cope with shifting conditions, which is especially important in these volatile and high turnover activities. Regional cities tend to offer superior connectivity, better infrastructure and a deeper labour pool than small cities and towns. These sorts of activities appear to have made an important contribution to recent employment growth in cities such as Liverpool, Newcastle, Sheffield, Glasgow and Manchester.

Certain cities also offer unique advantages to *consumers*, often with spinoffs for further growth through business and domestic tourism (Glaeser & Gottlieb, 2006; Jones, Williams, Coats, *et al.*, 2006). Some facilities are only available in large cities because they are not viable elsewhere, such as major entertainment venues, convention centres, museums, opera, art galleries or specialised centres of education and health. Rising overheads and exceptional costs of modernising such amenities in line with changes in fashion and technology may promote increasing concentration in the biggest centres. Cities also offer greater choice of shopping, restaurants, hotels, sporting facilities, social infrastructure and careers to attract people to visit, study, live and work. Growth in consumer services has been vital to the recovery of cities such as Birmingham, Manchester and Glasgow. Being at the centre of multimodal regional transport networks and having a large residential population within easy reach are major advantages for them over smaller, more isolated cities with centres that function less well, such as Stoke, Medway or Hull.

Consumer hubs are also reinforced by demographic changes such as smaller, dual-earner households, busier lifestyles and the expansion of higher education, which favour 'city living' (Costa & Kahn, 2000; Nathan & Urwin, 2005). The dense districts at the core of large cities enable more efficient and intense social interaction and better access to services and amenities than those available in smaller settlements. Outward commuting by people willing to pay a premium to live in central cities but working in surrounding areas indicates the consumption benefits gained. The growth of consumer hubs also coincides with the expansion of powerful multinationals in retailing, entertainment and hospitality that reap large internal scale economies, and that can afford to speculate on vacant and underused property, and therefore tend over time to displace smaller, independent enterprises from city centres. This threatens the diversity of their amenities and could undermine the special attractiveness of these cities, which is a challenge for policy. Part of the response may be to recognise the value of secondary property in off-centre locations and not completely neglect these places in terms of planning, infrastructure and public realm policies.

The Prospects for Sustained and Balanced Growth

Does the recent revival of many British cities provide the basis for continuing prosperity, accompanied by a progressive decline in worklessness, poverty and social distress? Before considering the likely effects of the new policy framework, it is important to outline some of the basic economic challenges.

Cities are bound to face a stronger headwind in the next few years – a deterioration in overall economic conditions, more cautious private investors, lower household expenditure and tighter public spending. Cities with a large consumer sector are particularly vulnerable to an economic downturn. City centres are likely to be hit harder than other areas by the credit squeeze and slump in the residential and commercial property markets. A contraction in new construction and a slowdown in discretionary consumer spending on entertainment, tourism and luxury goods will undermine jobs and the willingness of employers to participate in recruitment and training schemes. Looking further ahead, the boom in online internet services and mobile devices may impact on a range of activities that have helped to bolster city centres in recent years, including shopping, socialising and entertainment. The generation brought up with Google, eBay and Facebook may be more inclined to conduct some of their social interactions, professional collaborations, leisure pursuits and commercial purchases virtually in future.

Cities with large generic office services are less vulnerable to a slowdown in consumption, but face two significant concerns for the future. One is offshoring to lower cost locations, since many of these activities are sensitive to domestic labour and property costs. The other is technological change, including the potential for some of these services to become automated through new information and communications technologies. In both cases the pace of change is unclear, although there are sufficient examples available to indicate that they are real threats.

The knowledge hub is a seductive formula widely envisaged to cope with such eventualities (HM Treasury, 2006; Jones, Williams, Coats, *et al.*, 2006; Jones, Williams, Lee, *et al.*, 2006). It implies moving the economy up the value chain to more original, higher quality products and services that will protect and indeed enhance living standards over time, based on smart, professional, white collar occupations. It means continual change, creativity and innovation to find new ways of doing things and new things to do. And it depends on progressively raising skill levels and increasing the proportion of people entering further and higher education. But many questions arise.

Is this a feasible scenario for most cities? This depends on how broadly the knowledge hub is defined. If it is confined to advanced producer services and nascent industries it may be out of reach for cities with little established capacity in these sectors and no strong research institutions. You simply cannot build a sophisticated knowledge economy from scratch. There are also big risks of wasteful duplication if many cities focus on a small number of fashionable high-end sectors and functions. However, if the scope is widened across industry sectors, with a more general emphasis on developing capabilities for change and encouraging improvements over time through original analysis, experimentation, improvisation and upgrading of existing firms and related organisations, then it is much more realistic. Activities might include improving managerial competences and technical capabilities, enhancing products and services, building external trading relationships and adapting innovations created in other places. Some objectives might be quite simple, like responding more quickly to emerging opportunities by applying ideas and best practice from elsewhere.

There may be other assets to build upon too, including those associated with consumer hubs and generic services. Cities with appealing amenities, lifestyles and good external connections, arising from strengths in business or consumer tourism, may have some foundation from which to attract and retain people with different aptitudes, such as entrepreneurs. Cities with purposeful higher education institutions may have the means for building up the skills base, particularly from within but also by attracting students from elsewhere. Experience suggests that a coincidental increase in the demand for skills (in the form of rewarding jobs) is essential to avoid underemployment, frustrated aspirations and outmigration of the excess skilled population. Economic development policies have a vital role to play in improving local business conditions, strengthening firms' underlying competitiveness and helping them to diversify and develop new markets.

Another question is whether this is a sufficient scenario for cities? The answer again hinges partly on the breadth of definition, but also the functioning of the labour and housing markets and the impact of economic inequalities. The main risk is developing an imbalanced employment structure that is inaccessible to local residents – a skills mismatch. In Greater London, for example, the employment rate of working age residents is one of the lowest in the UK, despite the city's economic strengths. Shortages of affordable housing and childcare, plus a spatial mismatch between areas of job growth and worklessness, create multiple barriers to work for less-skilled workers (HM Treasury, 2007a). An unequal city with polarised labour and housing markets constrains upward mobility, limits life chances and is socially unstable. Highly specialised urban economies are also more vulnerable to economic instability associated with business cycles or external shocks afflicting their dominant industries, as with financial services in London.

Conclusion: The Central Dilemma for the New Policy for Cities

The government's positive interest in cities is justifiably widely welcomed, recognising that they present many of the country's greatest challenges and opportunities. Yet, there has been far more rhetoric surrounding a new policy for cities than actual delivery of new powers and resources. So there is also widespread recognition of much still to be done in terms of practical actions to make a difference. By way of conclusion, it is helpful to focus on one of the central dilemmas of the new spatial policy. The difficulty in negotiating this ambiguity is one of the reasons for the slow progress.

Underlying much of the SNR is a tension between promoting economic prosperity and reducing social inequality. There are different ways this is expressed elsewhere: economic growth and social justice; competitiveness and cohesion; efficiency and equity; wealth creation and distribution; opportunity and need. Each means slightly different things, but they allude to a common challenge for social democracies. Historically, spatial policy has sought to strike a balance between both goals, and ideally to find ways of combining them to avoid a simple trade-off. The 'Third Way' asserted that they go together and are mutually supportive – 'two sides of the same coin' (Buck *et al.*, 2005; Turok, 2006). A close reading of the SNR suggests more of a trade-off view of the world. Part of its purpose is to tilt the balance more towards the growth/efficiency side of the equation because spatial policy is thought to have been too concerned with social equality and to have had weak economic foundations.

At the neighbourhood level this is apparent in the tension between targeting the areas of greatest need and those with better prospects of revitalisation. At several points the SNR advocates a stronger focus on 'areas with the potential for sustainable economic growth' (p. 103; see also p. 75). Yet, this appears to be contradicted elsewhere: 'concentrate neighbourhood renewal funding more closely on the most deprived areas' (p. 8). An efficiency argument underlies the case for concentration as opposed to spreading the resources across deprived areas. Another illustration is the desire to shift the emphasis within regeneration from social welfare programmes towards economic development and worklessness.

There are similar dilemmas at the city-region level, between focusing on core cities as newfound drivers of contemporary growth, rather than older industrial towns, mining areas and rural market towns, many of which have lost their original rationale. At the interregional level, there are tensions between reinforcing the growth of the London/South-East agglomeration and encouraging development in the North. Labour market policy is split by parallel tensions. Should it help to raise the skills of existing workers and promote upward mobility in order to free up more entry-level jobs, or concentrate on getting workless groups into employment? Among people out of work, should the focus be on those who are most employable or those furthest from the labour market and facing multiple barriers?

There are no easy answers to these deep dilemmas. It is rarely a question of either/or. Economic development policy has always involved striking a balance, recognising the need for realism in what can be achieved. Effectiveness depends on sound judgements about what is possible in the circumstances. Conditions vary greatly between economic sectors, places and points in time, depending on prevailing forces and attitudes. A good evidence base can help by providing information on the relative costs and benefits of different options, informed by thoroughgoing public consultation.

There is a tendency in discussions about spatial policy to assume that making decisions at one scale is inherently superior to another, and even that there is a 'spatial fix' that can resolve these tensions. The SNR was set up partly to find the 'right' spatial level for economic regeneration policy, but it is ultimately ambivalent about this. Several think tanks and lobby groups are currently prone to present devolution to the city or city-region as a panacea (Centre for Cities, 2007; Gonzalez *et al.*, 2006). There are dangers in this, as the article has shown. Cities are not self-contained systems that can resolve deep-seated problems of worklessness and poverty on their own. More devolved powers and resources would certainly help improve the efficacy of city authorities, but there will be a continuing need for government involvement at all levels to increase prosperity and tackle inequalities.

Acknowledgements

Thanks are due to Lorraine Temple for her assistance with the data analysis and to Richard Cairns, Ines Newman and Trevor Davies for their comments on an earlier draft.

References

Buck, N., Gordon, I., Harding, A. & Turok, I. (2005) *Changing Cities: Rethinking Urban Competitiveness, Cohesion and Governance* (London: Palgrave).

Castells, M. (2000) *The Information Age: Economy, Society and Culture. Volume 1: The Rise of the Network Society*, 2nd edn. (Oxford: Blackwell).

Centre for Cities (2007) *Cities Outlook 2008* (London: Centre for Cities).

Costa, D. L. & Kahn, M. E. (2000) Power couples: Changes in locational choice of the college educated, 1940–1990, *Quarterly Journal of Economics*, 115(4), pp. 1287–1315.

Communities and Local Government (2007) *Economics Paper 1: A Framework for Intervention* (London: CLG).

Department of Communities and Local Government (2006) *Strong and Prosperous Communities: The Local Government White Paper* (London: DCLG).

Department of Environment, Transport and the Regions (1997) *Regeneration Programmes – The Way Forward.* Discussion Paper (London: DETR).

Department of Trade and Industry (2001) *Business Clusters in the UK – A First Assessment* (London: DTI).

Duranton, G. & Puga, D. (2004) Micro-foundations of urban agglomeration economies, in: V. Henderson & J. Thisse (Eds) *Handbook of Urban and Regional Economics*, Vol. 4, (Amsterdam: North Holland) pp. 2063–2117.

Eddington (2006) *The Eddington Transport Study* (London: HM Treasury).
European Commission (2007) *State of European Cities* (Brussels: Directorate-General Regional Policy).
Fingleton, B. (2003) Increasing returns: Evidence from local wage rates in Great Britain, *Oxford Economic Papers*, 55, pp. 716–739.
Fothergill, S. (2005) A new regional policy for Britain, *Regional Studies*, 39(5), pp. 659–667.
Glaeser, E. & Gottlieb, J. (2006) Urban resurgence and the consumer city, *Urban Studies*, 43(8), pp. 1275–1299.
Gonzalez, S., Tomaney, J. & Ward, N. (2006) Faith in the city-region?, *Town and Country Planning*, Nov., pp. 315–317.
Graham, D. (2006) *Investigating the Link between Agglomeration and Productivity for UK Industries* (London: Imperial College).
Hall, P. & Pain, K. (2006) *The Polycentric Metropolis* (London: Earthscan).
HM Treasury (2006) *The Importance of Cities to Regional Growth. Devolving Decision Making: 3 – Meeting the Regional Economic Challenge* (London: HM Treasury).
HM Treasury (2007a) *Employment Opportunity for All: Tackling Worklessness in London* (London: HM Treasury).
HM Treasury (2007b) *Review of Sub-national Economic Development and Regeneration* (London: HM Treasury).
Home Office (2001) *Community Cohesion: A Report of the Independent Review Team* (London: Home Office).
Jones, A., Williams, L., Coats, D., Lee, N. & O'Keeffe, A. (2006) *Enabling Cities in the Knowledge Economy* (London: Department of Communities and Local Government).
Jones, A., Williams, L., Lee, N., Coats, D. & Cowling, M. (2006) *Ideopolis: Knowledge City-Regions* (London: The Work Foundation).
Lawless, P. (2006) Area-based urban interventions: Rationale and outcomes: The New Deal for Communities Programme in England, *Urban Studies*, 43(11), pp. 1991–2011.
Lucci, P. & Seex, P. (2007) *London's Links: Who Benefits from London's Success?* (London: Centre for Cities).
Lupton, R. (2003) *Poverty Street: The Dynamics of Neighbourhood Decline and Renewal* (Bristol: Policy Press).
Marshall, A. & Webber, C. (2007) *The Case for Better Transport Investment: Agglomeration and Growth in the Leeds City-region* (London: Centre for Cities).
Nathan, M. & Urwin, C. (2005) *City People: City Centre Living in the UK* (London: IPPR Centre for Cities).
OECD (2006) *Building a Competitive City Region: The Case of Newcastle* (Paris: OECD).
Office of the Deputy Prime Minister (2003) *Sustainable Communities: Building for the Future* (London: ODPM).
Office of the Deputy Prime Minister (2004) *Assessing the Impacts of Spatial Interventions: Regeneration, Renewal and Regional Development. The 3Rs guidance* (London: ODPM).
Office of the Deputy Prime Minister (2005) *Sustainable Communities: Homes for All. A Five Year Plan from the ODPM* (London: ODPM).
Parkinson, M., Champion, T., Evans, R., *et al.* (2006) *State of the English Cities* (London: Office of the Deputy Prime Minister).
Parr, J. B. (2005) Perspectives on the City-Region, *Regional Studies*, 39, pp. 555–566.
Pascal, A. (1987) The vanishing city, *Urban Studies*, 24(6), pp. 597–603.
Prime Minister's Strategy Unit (2005) *Improving the Prospects of People Living in Areas of Multiple Deprivation in England* (London: PMSU).
Rice, P., Venables, A. & Patacchini, E. (2006) Spatial determinants of productivity: Analysis for the regions of Great Britain, *Regional Science and Urban Economics*, 36, pp. 727–752.
Rosenthal, S. & Strange, W. (2004) Evidence on the nature and sources of agglomeration economies, in: V. Henderson & J. Thisse (Eds) *Handbook of Urban and Regional Economics, Vol. 4*, pp. 2119–2171 (Amsterdam: North Holland).
Sanderson, I. (2006) *Worklessness in Deprived Neighbourhoods: A Review of the Evidence* (London: Department for Communities and Local Government).

Scottish Executive (2006) *People and Place: Regeneration Policy Statement* (Edinburgh: Scottish Executive).

Storper, M. & Manville, M. (2006) Behaviour, preferences and cities: Urban theory and urban resurgence, *Urban Studies*, 43(8), pp. 1247–1274.

Turok, I. (2004) Cities, regions and competitiveness, *Regional Studies*, 38(9), pp. 1069–1083.

Turok, I. (2006) The connections between social cohesion and city competitiveness, *Competitive Cities in the Global Economy*, pp. 353–366 (Paris: OECD).

Turok, I. (2007a) Full employment strategies for cities: The case of Glasgow, *OECD Papers*, 6(12), pp. 214–231.

Turok, I. (2007b) Urban policy in Scotland: New conventional wisdom, old problems?, in: M. Keating (Ed) *Social Democracy in Scotland*, pp. 141–168 (Brussels: Peter Lang).

Turok, I. & Edge, N. (1999) *The Jobs Gap in Britain's Cities: Employment Loss and Labour Market Consequences* (Bristol: Policy Press).

Turok, I., Kearns, A., Fitch, D., *et al.* (2006) *State of the English Cities: Social Cohesion* (London: Department of Communities and Local Government).

Turok, I. & Mykhnenko, V. (2008) Resurgent European Cities?, *Urban Research and Practice: Journal of the European Urban Research Association*, 1(1), pp. 54–77.

Turok, I. & Robson, B. (2007) Linking neighbourhood regeneration to city-region growth: Why and how?, *Journal of Urban Regeneration and Renewal*, 1(1), pp. 44–54.

Webster, D. (2006) Welfare reform: Facing up to the geography of worklessness, *Local Economy*, 21(2), pp. 107–116.

FEATURES

Reflexive Local and Regional Economic Development and International Policy Transfer

GRAHAM HAUGHTON & RACHEL NAYLOR

ABSTRACT This article looks at the international dimension of local and regional economic development policy. We illustrate our argument about the difficulties of comparing the relative effectiveness of policy using the experience of a comparative study of local and regional economic development in Australia, the US, England and Northern Ireland. The empirical work suggests that the preferred tools of local economic development and their locally perceived effectiveness vary but that careful interpretation is necessary to understand why this is the case. Given that international policy exchange is neither inherently bad nor good, but that it is inevitable, we argue for further exploration of the process of cross-national policy transfer to ensure we are learning appropriate lessons.

State Restructuring, Competitive Policy and Policy Transfer

Local and regional economic development has continued to attract considerable governmental support and investment in recent years, perhaps disguised from initial view by the proliferation of scales now involved. In the case of England this involves neighbourhoods, local governments, sub-regions, city-regions, regions and meta-regions such as the Northern Way, which have all at various times in the past decade been presented as the preferred scale for public policy interventions.

Geddes and Newman (1999) spoke presciently of the dangers of the new regional structures 'replaying the problems of the business-led experiment of the second half of the 1990s' (p. 17). It is certainly a concern that in practice central government has continued to provide more powers and resources to Regional Development Agencies (RDAs), but with clear expectations that they use these to address government priorities, as expressed in Public Service Agreements. The result is that far from being sources of innovative policy ideas, RDAs are little more than agents of government working in the same prescriptive and restrictive style when it comes to funding local economic development. The locus of power may have shifted somewhat, but the methods barely changed.[1] Again, this was perhaps predicted by Geddes and Newman when they posited a future scenario where 'Powerful regional institutions, closely linked to central government and the EU and to business, would continue to submerge local economic development in an ever more amorphous "regeneration" policy' (p. 23).

The allocation of substantial sums for sub-national economic development initiatives is embedded within the contradictory politics of western governments tending to argue that in an era of globalisation they are powerless to intervene against the grain of market forces, whilst presenting sub-national governmental bodies with the task of restructuring to compete in the global market place. Given this central contradiction, it is convenient for both central government and local actors to claim that local and regional agencies are more flexible, locally sensitised and therefore better placed to steer the economic development of their areas. Where they disagree is in the approach to local autonomy and the levels of funding required for local agencies to make a difference to their local economies.

In the broader context of a central government and Regional Development Agency predisposition to fund local agencies at arms'-length through short-term programmes, valuing experimentations and competitive bidding for funds over consistent support, the search for 'new' approaches is endemic in local economic development circles. Forced to compete for regional, national and EU funding whose rules of engagement prioritise innovation and 'exit strategies', practitioners have little option but to scour the horizon in search of new ideas in the hope of gaining favour from funding bodies. The remnants remain for all to see: business parks, science parks, incubators, enterprise zones, credit unions, LETS, training centres, cultural quarters, big events (garden festivals, world student games) and of course all the work on picking business winners, variously branded as being about clusters, sectors and supply chains.

---

[1] We know that Regional Development Agencies and their supporters would dispute this. With no meaningful regional democratic accountability and tight central budgetary control, RDAs do what they are contractually required to do. Our view is that current reform proposals to hand further powers to RDAs will turn them into much unloved regional monopolies, not unlike the late and largely unlamented TECs, which swaggered to their demise gathering new powers from a fading government, whilst their attempts to improve their accountability struggled to convince many (Hart *et al.*, 1996).

The successes are there of course, along with the empty and half-used infrastructure of the failures.[2]

Internationalisation and Policy Transfer

One of the most distinctive features of UK local economic development practice is its international openness, embracing a widespread desire to engage with ideas from elsewhere, evident in the importance of European networking activity in many local economic departments and, to a lesser extent, other agencies (Lefèvre & d'Algergo, 2007). Partly attracted and stimulated by European funding of course, these new institutional assemblages also offer genuine opportunities for opening up creative discussions with others and bringing about new insights and possibilities for strengthening local economies.

As well as the benefits from such openness, there are dangers of falling for the latest fad and attempting to transfer ideas from one national context to another, generating some interesting academic debates, not least around the practices sometimes known as 'the new regionalism' (Lovering, 1999; MacLeod, 2001). In new regionalism the region is seen as the appropriate scale to deploy development strategies encouraging local and regional actors across all sectors to cooperate in order to boost business competitiveness and employment levels. These strategies are influenced by powerful narratives about the successes to be derived from business 'clustering', actor networking, strengthened social and cultural capital and so on. Initially rooted in debates on flexible specialisation, later in notions of intelligent regions (Geddes & Newman, 1999), this work drew selectively in interpretations of economic development trajectories in prototypical regions such as Emilia-Romagna in Italy and Silicon Valley in California. Geddes and Newman (1999) noted how difficult it was proving to transfer some of these ideas to the UK (p. 14) and wrote of the wishful thinking already apparent in some analyses (p. 17). Not surprisingly, the conceptual and empirical problems associated with the new regionalist approach have continued to be debated, amidst claims that some regional success stories have been overplayed and taken out of context as providing some form of universal solution to local economic problems (Lovering, 1999; MacLeod, 2001).

Though such criticisms are perhaps most notable for the large-scale projects, the example of LETS, another imported policy idea, suggests that community-based approaches are similarly likely to be eagerly embraced only to be found wanting in various ways when it comes to implementation. Critiques of LETS have pointed out that they tend be sustainable in areas which are already affluent such as Stroud in England (Aldridge *et al.*,

---

[2] A national audit of such un- and underused assets and other evidence might help address the chronic policy amnesia and tendency to overexaggerate likely future impacts when putting in funding bids (see Flyvbjerg, 2006).

2003) and Banbridge in Northern Ireland. As economic development schemes they appear to be less successful. Writing of Hounslow LETS, a scheme set up by the local authority attempting economic regeneration, Aldridge and Patterson (2002) note the scheme, like many others, shows there are disappointingly few transactions. In Northern Ireland, where the Rural Development Council set up LETS systems in areas of disadvantage, these were not sustained after development workers' contracts ended. Aldridge and Patterson (p. 371) argue that it was the 'widespread uncritical promotion of LETS' potential' that was responsible for their rapid growth. The number of LETS schemes has declined markedly in the 2000s (LETSLink UK, 2008).

Notwithstanding such debates about the potential pitfalls, international policy transfer remains one of the emblematic tendencies within the current phase of capitalist development, with actors borrowing ideas widely, but selectively, and adapting them, but not necessarily sensitively (Jessop, 2000; Peck 2002). This approach has been encouraged through government-funded research on policies elsewhere, bringing in overseas advisors and 'gurus' to speak at conferences, and of course through EU funded initiatives. For instance LEADER programmes (French acronym for Links between Actions for the Development of the Rural Economy) receive European structural fund support local public–private–voluntary partnerships to develop innovative approaches to boost economic development. Those involved are expected to share ideas with other such local agencies across the EU via a central observatory, the web, bulletins and conferences. Some interlocal and international cooperation between such groups is also assisted under LEADER.

Driven by a combination of broad structural tendencies, competitive funding regimes and specific programmes for policy exchange, local economic development agencies are engaged on an unceasing quest for the new approach that will provide 'value-added'. One consequence of this has been an unholy alliance between 'fast' policy transfer, rapid evaluation and judgements, and a rush to replace and reinvent. Far from the 'studied agnosticism and empiricism as to what policy solutions... work best' imagined by Geddes and Newman (1999, p. 19), there has been a pseudoagnosticism and highly selective empiricism, where central government has been very active in choosing what criteria it is willing to endorse in judging the success of the projects it funds. Whilst New Labour talks of a pragmatic approach to backing whatever can be proven to work, the experience with initiatives such as Prototype Employment Zones where decisions on what aspects of a policy would be deemed appropriate for future 'rollout' emerged before the results of the official evaluation (Haughton *et al.*, 2000a, 2000b; Jones & Gray, 2001). This turbulent operating environment brings with it a distinctive set of attributes across the sector, not least funding uncertainties and huge amounts of time spent on bidding for short-term funding from fickle government sources (Peck, 2001, 2002). There is rather less time and money spent on looking at international comparative research on local economic development to find out which policies local practitioners think work best and that might explain why policies set out in one context might not work in another.

Faltering Footsteps towards Integrated International Comparative Research

There have been attempts to engage in international comparisons of local economic development practices in the past, often bilateral comparison, sometimes bringing together research findings from different studies using somewhat different research instruments rather than generating comparable data (Geddes, 2005; Wiewel & Hall, 1992; Wolman & Stoker, 1992).

Seeking to address some of these concerns about comparative local economic development research, we recently worked with a group of colleagues to try to identify what local economic development meant in each of the differing contexts of Australia, England, Northern Ireland and the USA, including what practitioners felt worked best for them, and what worked least effectively. The tables presented here give a brief taster of these findings (see Beer *et al.*, 2003, 2005, for more detailed findings and analysis). Reflecting the growing diversity of actors involved in local economic development, we included within our sampling frame not simply local governments, but also other key actors, such as Business Links and LSCs in the case of England, community economic development organisations in Northern Ireland. This created some asymmetries, as did the sheer size of the task in the USA, which meant we necessarily had to adopt a sampling approach rather than attempting to contact all possible respondents. In the end, we sent out 3777 questionnaires and received 968 usable responses. As expected we found differences between the nations and also some evidence of convergence over time, recognising the rapidity of policy transfer in recent years.

The most distinctive findings perhaps concerned the strong differences that emerged in what local economic development aspired to be, in terms of overriding objectives, and with this the variation in approaches adopted. For instance the pursuit of economic growth and increased employment was clearly dominant for US respondents, those in England were more likely to focus on particular target groups, such as those living in disadvantaged areas, whilst in Australia a strong emphasis exists on retaining population, a real issue in some rural areas, and on advocacy activities (Table 1). In Northern Ireland, the most distinctive features were the emphasis on broader quality of life objectives, and stimulating the involvement of local people and entrepreneurs, possibly reflecting the high numbers of community organisations in the sample.

We made a distinction between 'business-related' (Table 2) and 'regional capacity making' (Table 3) activities and asked respondents to tell us what types of actions they had supported over the previous year, to get a sense of any national differences in 'mainstream' local economic development

Table 1. Percentage of agencies reporting adoption of nominated objectives

Objective	Australia	England	US	Northern Ireland
Promote economic growth	81	74	93	65
Increase local incomes	26	35	51	33
Promote employment growth	65	48	75	58
Improve the quality of life of regional/local communities	68	61	67	79
Regenerate/revitalise regional/local economy	54	67	55	61
Diversify regional/local economy	48	42	63	33
Protect/increase revenue base of local government	35	9	46	6
Retain/increase regional/local population	44	12	27	27
Attract/recruit new businesses	61	47	75	41
Develop local businesses (start-ups, expansion, retention)	54	58	72	47
Build local partnerships between public agencies, private sector and community	61	66	56	69
Stimulate involvement of local people and entrepreneurs	50	44	39	68
Build capacity of the region/local area for development	53	37	54	44
Improve employment, incomes, welfare of disadvantaged groups	27	58	35	67
Promote environmentally sustainable regional/local economy	53	46	32	44
Advocate for/lobby governments on behalf of region/local area	57	40	26	41

activities. Although a slightly blunt tool, it did reveal some interesting findings. Place marketing emerges as one of the most widely used tools, yet as a later table will reveal, efforts aimed at inward investment and marketing also emerged as one of the least effective tools used by agencies when they assessed themselves (see Table 4). Given the supposed emphasis on 'evidence-based policy', this contradiction merits some further exploration – and explanation! This could be explored in future research through the use of comparative in-depth qualitative interviewing, for example.

In general, it looks as if English agencies were particularly addicted to 'new regionalist' inspired forms of intervention, for instance work on industry clusters, supply chains and business clusters.

When it comes to regional capacity building, focusing mainly on the English case, the most startling difference is the relatively low attention paid to ensuring adequate infrastructure was in place. One argument might be that other agencies are perfectly capable of providing for such activities. The other argument is that a look at any English city shows the true consequences of underattention to basic infrastructure issues.

Table 2. Percentage of agencies reporting participation in business-related assistance within the previous two years

Function performed	Australia	England	US	Northern Ireland
Marketing the region and its facilities to prospective businesses	78	68	86	49
Operating a business incubator	20	43	19	27
Operating industrial estates or science parks	21	48	29	19
Other provision of land or buildings	40	55	45	26
If you are a government agency, offering reduced government rates, taxes or charges to attract or retain business	23	13	32	0
Subsidising relocation costs for businesses moving to the region	10	9	18	3
Assisting businesses with training or recruitment of labour	36	68	58	38
If you are a government agency, providing streamlined approval/development processes	39	9	27	0
Coordinating the activities of public sector agencies to support business development	51	73	69	28
Providing general small and medium enterprise business support programmes	46	70	53	48
Assisting firms to access venture capital	25	24	37	20
Providing information on programmes of government departments and other agencies	74	69	81	58
Assistance in accessing funding and support services from governments at all levels	75	71	72	63
Assistance with technology transfer/ innovation	31	33	35	33
Assisting firms to meet quality standards, whether those of their customers or ISO standards	14	27	15	14
Assistance, either financial or advisory, with marketing nationally	39	36	40	26
Assistance, either financial or advisory, with marketing internationally	21	26	20	20
Promoting supply chain associations	23	42	8	16
Assisting the development of industry clusters	36	56	33	24
Tourism promotion	74	64	56	46
Assistance with major or special events in the region	82	64	58	63
Urban business district development (Main Street)	62	33	54	25
Programmes to help people establish their own small business	44	65	52	53
Other local employment creation programmes	55	62	45	60

Table 3. Percentage of agencies reporting participation in nominated forms of regional capacity building within the previous two years

Function performed	Australia	England	US	Northern Ireland
Improvement of regional/local physical infrastructure (e.g. roads, railways utilities)	73	49	79	25
Improvement of regional/local tele-communications infrastructure	55	23	51	8
Improvement of regional/local service provision (such as education or medical services)	50	50	36	33
Development of planning for business sites and premises	50	65	73	28
Education and training for youth not targeted to a specific firm/enterprise/business	37	66	32	58
Education and training for minority groups not targeted to a specific firm/enterprise/ business	24	53	22	23
Education and training in general not targeted to a specific firm/enterprise/business	34	69	42	56
Improving regional/local economic development strategic planning and implementation capacity	71	72	81	51
Analysis of the regional/local economy	61	80	67	47
Developing cooperation and networking between firms and relevant public and private sector agencies and institutions	58	68	62	49
Coordinating government programmes	55	63	61	25
Acting as a lobbyist for the region/local area with governments	70	60	46	43
Identification of business opportunities or gaps in the regional/local economy and implementation of strategies to fill them	54	51	51	46
Attempting to influence land use regulations and planning decisions that impact on business	45	43	49	19

Also distinctive is the English emphasis on various forms of education and training activity, reflecting longstanding debates on 'skills mismatch' plus the nature of subcontracting for these activities. Networking and other governance activities are also strongly represented in England, again reflecting a 'new regionalist' emphasis on networking and capacity building. It also reflects the 'integration' agenda of recent British governments, to improve joined up policy making. It may actually be the case that it is precisely this approach that means direct engagement with lobbying for infrastructural improvements stands out less in the English case.

Table 4. Five most commonly reported most and least effective activities or strategies

Rank	Most effective activity	% respondents[a]	Rank	Least effective activity	% respondents[a]
Australia			*Australia*		
1	Business support/advice	21	1	Other	16
2	Infrastructure development/service provision	15	2	Inward investment/promotion of region	14
3	Networking/partnerships	14	3	Some types of business assistance	10
4	Sector planning/development	10	4	Land preparation/site/premises development	6
5	Tourism promotion/special events	10	5	Training skills/labour market programmes	5
England			*England*		
1	Business support/advice	23	1	Inward investment/promotion of region	24
2	Training skills/labour market programmes	18	2	Other	16
3	Land preparation/site/premises development	10	3	Can't say, unable to determine	11
4	Networking/partnerships	10	4	Training skills/labour market programmes	7
5	Inward investment/promoting the region	10	5	Business support/advice	7
US			*US*		
1	Business support/advice	19	1	Marketing generally	22
2	Land preparation/site/premises development	16	2	Inward investment/promoting the region	18
3	Provision of grants or loans for development (including to businesses)	15	3	Other	17
4	Networking/partnerships	13	4	Some types of business assistance	6
5	Inward investment/promoting the region	11	5	Business support/advice	5
Northern Ireland			*Northern Ireland*		
1	Business support/advice	27	1	Other	32
2	Training skills/labour market programmes	24	2	None	7
3	Working with the community sector	19	3	Working with the community sector	7
4	Networking/partnerships	14	4	Inward investment/promoting the region	4
5	Managed workspaces/business incubators	10	5	Tourism promotion/special events	4

Note: [a]Percentage of respondents to include this activity as one of their responses.

Table 5. Most significant impediments to agency effectiveness

Rank	Impediment	% of respondents[a]
Australia		
1	Insufficient untied funding to use as leverage with other agencies	60.2
2	Lack of funding for core business	60.1
3	Short duration of much of the funding	53.2
4	Too much staff time spent seeking funding	48.5
5	Priorities of funders have more influence on organisation than region's needs	47.4
England		
1	Short duration of much of the funding	65.2
2	Inflexible rules and guidelines of funders	59.5
3	Insufficient untied funding to use as leverage with other agencies	54.9
4	Lack of funding for core business	52.7
5	Priorities of funders have more influence on organisation than region's needs	48.6
US		
1	Lack of funding for core business	45.2
2	Insufficient untied funding to use as leverage with other agencies	41.3
3	Short duration of much of the funding	36.1
4	Priorities of funders have more influence on organisation than region's needs	29.3
5	Inflexible rules and guidelines of funders	28.9
Northern Ireland		
1	Short duration of much of the funding	80.7
2	Lack of funding for core business	69.4
3	Inflexible rules and guidelines of funders	67.9
4	Too much staff time spent seeking funding	67.6
5	Insufficient untied funding to use as leverage with other agencies	65.7

Note: [a]Percentage of respondents agreeing that each represents an impediment.

Table 4 is interesting, revealing the five main 'successes' and relative failures perceived by respondents in each territory. Business support activities come out top in each case study area. Networking also appears in the top five for each case study. So there is a good degree of commonality here. Asking our respondents to identify the main impediments to their being more successful (Table 5), we would argue that all but one of the top five responses in each case study area were actually problems of governance. The exception is the lack of core funding, though arguably this too is more than simply the usual complaint about lack of money and more a concern that fragmented governance brings with it fragmentary funding. All the other responses more or less hint at the same set of interrelated problems, namely that the core business of running an economic development organisation was increasingly concerned with competitive bidding for funds and working effectively with others. Rather ironically, the main impediment to effective local economic development appears to be the very apparatus that seeks to foster innovation, rapid policy transfer and monitoring for effectiveness.

Lessons for the Future

For all the potential pitfalls of international comparative research on local economic development, it remains an important part of the future research agenda if we are truly to understand how ideas emerge and get translated into other contexts. An important part of the future agenda for local economic development practice and research should be to find a workable comparative analytical and methodological framework for international comparative work on the effectiveness of different governance structures, for identifying which policy approaches work best, both in isolation and, most importantly, in combination. Given the problems of uncritical policy exchange, attention will need to be given to the specific political and economic contexts of different areas, and their respective institutional histories, past learning and future aspirations. The challenge is to develop an evidence base that shows how well different approaches work in similar forms of governance system, and over and above this whether particular approaches work best within particular governance systems.

Acknowledgements

We would like to thank our colleagues in the research project reported on here, Andrew Beer, Terry Clower, Alaric Maude, Terry Robson, and to acknowledge the generous funding of the South Australian Local Government Association.

References

Aldridge, T. J. & Patterson, A. (2002) LETS get real: Constraints on the development of Local Exchange Trading Schemes, *Area*, 34(4), pp. 370–381.

Aldridge, T. J., Patterson, A. & Tooke, J. (2003) Trading places: geography and the role of LETS in local sustainable development, in: S. Buckingham & K. S. Theobald (Eds) *Local Environmental Sustainability*, pp. 169–194 (Cambridge: Woodhead).

Beer, A., Clower, T., Haughton, G. & Maude, A. (2005) Neoliberalism and the institutions for regional development in Australia, *Geographical Research*, 43(1), pp. 40–58.

Beer, A., Haughton, G., & Maude, A. (Eds) (2003) *Developing Locally: Lessons in Economic Development from Four Nations* (Bristol: Policy Press).

Flyvbjerg, B. (2006) From Nobel Prize to project management: Getting risks right, *Project Management Journal*, 37(3), pp. 5–15.

Geddes, M. (2005) Local governance under neoliberalism: International perspectives, *Policy Studies*, 26, pp. 359–378.

Geddes, M. & Newman, I. (1999) Evolution and conflict in local economic developement, *Local Economy*, 13(5), pp. 12–15.

Hart, T., Haughton, G. & Peck, J. (1996) Accountability and the non-elected local state: Bringing Training and Enterprise Councils to local account, *Regional Studies*, 30(4), pp. 429–441.

Haughton, G., Peck, J., Tickell, A., Jones, M., Littlewood, S. & While, A. (2000a) *A Qualitative and Contextual Evaluation of Prototype Employment Zones* (London: DfEE).

Haughton, G., Jones, M., Peck, J., Tickell, A. & While, A. (2000) Labour Market policy as flexible welfare: prototype employment zones and the new workfarism, *Regional Studies*, 34(7), pp. 669–680.

Jessop, B. (2000) The crisis of the national spatio-temporal fix and the ecological dominance of globalizing, *International Journal of Urban and Regional Research*, 24(2), pp. 323–360.

Jones, M. & Gray, A. (2001) Social capital, or local workfarism? Reflections on Employment Zones, *Local Economy*, 16(3), pp. 178–186.

Lefèvre, C., & d'Algergo, E. (Guest Eds) (2007) International strategies of cities, explaining divergence and convergence, *Environment and Planning C*, 25(Whole No. 3), pp. 317–409.

Letslink UK (2008) Available at http://www.letslinkuk.net (accessed 11 Jan. 2008).

Lovering, J. (1999) Theory led by policy: The inadequacies of the new regionalism, *International Journal of Urban and Regional Research*, 23, pp. 379–395.

Macleod, G. (2001) New regionalism reconsidered: Globalisation and the remaking of political economic space, *International Journal of Urban and Regional Research*, 25(4), pp. 804–829.

Peck, J. (2001) Neoliberalizing states: Thin policies/hard outcomes, *Progress in Human Geography*, 25(3), pp. 445–455.

Peck, J. (2002) Political economies of scale: Fast policy, interscalar relations, and neoliberal workfare, *Economic Geography*, 78(3), pp. 331–360.

Wiewel, W. & Hall, C. (1992) Economic development: A Review of the British and US comparative literature, *Economic Development Quarterly*, 6, pp. 396–405.

Wolman, H. & Stoker, G. (1992) Understanding local economic development in a comparative context, *Economic Development Quarterly*, 6, pp. 406–417.

Reflections of a Torontonian in Sheffield

IAN BROMLEY

It has been 18 months since I accepted a job to head up a new economic development company in Sheffield, and 16 months since I moved my family of five from Toronto to Sheffield. Having worked in management consulting, at city and provincial governments in Toronto and across Ontario, having spent about six months in the UK over the course of my 43 years, and having done economic development advisory work in China, Japan, Brazil, the US and New Zealand, I expected that nothing I encountered would be all that new or different.

Our experience in Sheffield has been wonderful. Professionally I have been fortunate to have focused leadership in the City, national government support for City Development Companies (of which we were the first), and the opportunity to build a great team of people (I think one of the best teams in the UK or anywhere). I also have been fortunate to come to a city that really believes in economic development. After years of languishing as other core cities moved ahead, in the past ten years Sheffielders have seen their city centre transformed, and have enjoyed an economy with the fourth highest job growth rate in England.

On the personal side, Sheffield really is a very friendly and welcoming place (quite surprising really, given that it never had the population inflows and outflows of some of the more historically trade-related cities such as Liverpool or Leeds). My family is very happy here and we all enjoy our regular hikes into the fantastically beautiful Peak District, literally on our doorstep.

What I offer below are some reflections on some of the differences I've encountered as an ED practitioner moving from Canada to Northern England. None of it is meant to be critical of any individuals, institutions or policy choices.

Local Choice versus the 'Postcode Lottery'

The thought of a 'postcode lottery' stokes outrage amongst journalists and strikes fear into the hearts of politicians throughout Britain. It is a phrase and even a concept that is almost unknown in North America. The thought that public services might be different in different parts of Canada is not a big deal. Healthcare coverage for example varies across the ten provinces, and social supports and local tax levels vary considerably between cities within the same province. Most people in Ontario couldn't care less if Quebecers choose to pay higher income taxes in return for increased spending on childcare or more highly subsidised prescription drugs. Likewise, people can choose to live in a higher taxed, higher density urban environment, such as Toronto, which supports public transit and very good public services, or in the Town of Milton, 15 miles from the Toronto boundary, which offers lower taxes, fewer libraries and little public transport to speak of. This is called local choice and is considered a very good thing where I come from.

Centralisation and 'Regional Policy'

I knew that England was a very centralised country but I really did not grasp just how centralised it is, politically and geographically. Not only is politics and public policy concentrated at the national level (perhaps a function of the aversion to local choice), but the national transport networks radiate from London, the business decision makers are almost all in London, and the media is unbelievably concentrated there. In Toronto we had seven local TV stations, five local daily newspapers and about two dozen local radio stations. In Sheffield we have one daily tabloid paper and two radio stations.

London is a fantastic, dynamic, diverse global city and a great asset to the UK. The concentration of the UK's commercial, financial and transportation assets has been critical in achieving London's position as a global city. In contrast, Canada erodes its global competitive position by not supporting its major cities and trying to spread its relatively small economy equally across the country's massive geography. In this respect, my home and adopted countries sit at opposite ends of a spectrum.

I would expect that Canada could do with a fair bit more economic concentration and England with somewhat less. London is, and, barring any silly changes to tax codes or regulatory regimes, will remain, a global city. Investments in other parts of the country that could play a national, rather than necessarily global, economic role, would be wise in my view. Regional policy in England seems trapped in a London versus the rest model. Northern cities complain that London gets everything. London complains that the rest are laggards and welfare cases supported by London money. The whole debate needs to be recast.

Performance Indicators and Local Accountability

One of the difficulties of the concentration of public resources and political power is that central government departments, understandably, are not close enough to the ground to see what is really providing value for money. Very understandably, those departments feel compelled to develop intricate systems of performance measurement. In Sheffield's case we get support for economic development from Brussels through our Regional Development Agency, direct support from central government or national agencies, and national resources through the Regional Development Agency. In most cases the European or national agencies contract with the regional agencies, applying targets for outputs and outcomes, and cities then contract with regional agencies, applying targets for outputs and outcomes. All of this involves a lot of targets and boxes to tick, lots of European, national and regional strategies, funding bids, business plans, accountancy for results etc.

One perverse result of all of this is that consultants make gobs of money writing business plans, strategies and investment bids, then make gobs more evaluating business plans, strategies and investment bids, then make gobs more developing reports to account for the outcomes and outputs of those business plans, strategies and investment bids. Maybe I'm just cynical because after 16 months I'm still not clear on the difference between an output and an outcome.

Don't get me wrong – I fully accept that any publicly supported entity should have to prove its worth and report its results. But, on the ground, I meet daily with local political, business and community leaders, and ultimately they will judge our company's success or failure based on what they see and feel, not on the accountancy of performance indicators. Being closer to the ground we have accountability to local people, and have less need for performance accountancy to tell us what is working or not.

Smart Growth

Given the population density of this country, it is incredible to a North American how much green and open countryside remains. If England were developed with the same patterns as North America it would be one enormous suburban sprawl from Cornwall to Northumbria, with nothing but shopping malls, motorways and housing subdivisions. In my view, the English approach to land use policy is entirely better. I know that some blame greenbelts for high housing prices, but my hunch is that speculation has more to do with current house prices than policies that prevent developers from gobbling up the countryside.

Experimentation and Stability

The pace of change at the sub-national level is much slower where I come from. Things are pretty comfortable in the colonies, and naturally people don't want change when everything is comfortable. Here in the 'old country' in just the past 16 months I have seen changes to county and city council governance structures, the movement towards city regions, the introduction of new institutions (city development companies) and tools (LABVs, SBRs), and a sub-national review and three Secretaries of State/Deputy Prime Ministers with responsibility for communities and regions. It certainly provides an exciting and dynamic environment. However, economic development, place making and city building are long-term processes and require a certain amount of sustained effort and stability.

Local Taxation and Tax-base Competition

In North America, and particularly in some parts of the US, competition between neighbouring authorities for property tax base is relentless and destructive. In a region like Pittsburgh, with over 100 local authorities, municipal and local economic development is less about growing the region's economy than it is about making sure that your authority gets its fair share of development and, by extension property taxes. This results in bad planning and land use decisions, and often makes it impossible for neighbouring authorities to cooperate. I much prefer working in an atmosphere where we have every reason to work together with other authorities in our region to bring jobs and higher incomes to the region, not just to the city. Sheffield is transforming into a commercial and urban economy – it can no longer offer massive properties for industrial tenants. But our neighbours in South Yorkshire and the northern East Midlands do have plentiful land. We have everything to gain from working together.

In England, the downside of the centralisation of local taxation, and particularly of local business taxation, is that city councils have little financial incentive to work hard at attracting and retaining business. Schemes such as the LABGI have created some incentives for local councils, but are quite small and are being phased out. How do we find a middle position, which creates the right incentives to be business-friendly without creating the wrong incentives to adopt beggar-thy-neighbour tax base competition?

IN PERSPECTIVE

Sub-regional Economic Development – Consolidation and Culture

JOHN BERRY

In the run up to Gordon Brown's ascent into the premiership, there was a welter of policy reviews and White Papers, many of which will have a profound effect on economic development and regeneration work over the next few years. However we have yet to see how these various reviews of policy (Lyons, Sub-national review, Barker, Leitch etc) join up together to form a coherent economic narrative for the UK and there is also a sense that many of these policy reviews are pulling in opposite directions, with some confusion on leadership and focus. For instance are elements of our national (micro)economic policy, employer led or public sector led? Indeed do we have a joined up national economic strategy (as opposed to macroeconomic management) at all? Where do all the national government departments join together with the private and community sectors to produce the equivalent of a regional or sub-regional economic strategy? Perhaps if there was at least an attempt to draw some cross departmental thoughts together on such a national economic policy document, we would all be a little clearer on what we are trying to achieve rather than the current jumble of silo-ed service provision and new initiatives.

However there are some encouraging signs that national departments are beginning to move away from the trend of centralised control, management through national 'Next Steps' agencies and the Blairite obsession with the private sector in the delivery of required public sector outcomes. Even more exciting for local economy advocates and practitioners is the mood music that suggests that strategic local authorities and their local partners will be asked to take on greater responsibility for bringing the variety of policy agendas together at local level with the benefit of local democracy and better and more wide ranging partner engagement. However, this policy thread still has to be turned into a set of propositions and practice by local actors operating within a new settlement between central and local governance. So what are the principles that underlie the making of new propositions and practice for local authorities and economic development organisations in this new environment?

First, such a direction of travel puts a big responsibility on local authorities and their strategic partners to arrive at the structures and organisations that will allow such devolution and responsibility to occur. We have come a long way from the central civil servant view that local authorities and other local organisations are not to be trusted, which seemed to stem originally from Derek Hatton's Liverpool. Indeed I remember asking a civil servant, in the middle of a visit to a small safe country town in Cornwall in the early 1990s, why Cornwall County Council could not be trusted with some new development money, and being told it was 'because of Liverpool'. Even today there is a need to take further steps to convince government that local authorities and their partners are as effective at delivery as other mechanisms. One way of achieving this is through some structural consolidation of capacity at local level. Cornwall authorities are considering whether to do this under the new LAA framework being prepared for 2008.

Economic and regeneration development departments sit in three alternative places within strategic local authorities. In more prosperous areas the department is often situated in the Chief Executive department to remain close to the place shaping and policy agendas. In other authorities it is part of the planning/transportation/environment department usefully linking with other policy drivers. Where there is a wider range or greater amount of service delivery required, and a need to engage strongly with external partners, then a stand alone delivery organisation led by the local authority is becoming more common. These latter organisations provide a potential vehicle through which local authorities can convince central government that it has the capacity to deliver at local level.

Economic development and regeneration workers are usually spread in a wide variety of different organisations with different ownerships, focus and leadership. There is a very strong argument that more should be done at sub-regional and strategic local authority level to bring together groups of professions and functions within one or at least a very limited number of organisations. This agglomeration of functions has been happening at regional level with the Government's policy of building the breadth of responsibilities of the RDAs to include physical regeneration, funding projects, business support, skills and workforce development, local regeneration, tourism, arts etc. The emergence of City Development Companies and a patchwork of similar organisations in non-city environments is a response to this need which should be welcomed and encouraged. But this coordinated organisational framework also needs government commitment to ensure that different strands of policy take account of local governance. The Sub-National Review of Economic Development is an encouraging recognition of this need, although the Business Support simplification agenda and the continuing centralisation of some government departments and some RDAs runs counter to this direction of travel. A recent example for Cornwall of this continued centralisation is the approximate £250 million that is to be spent by DEFRA's Rural Development Programme for England (RDPE) in Cornwall over the next seven years. Only about £2.75 million of that sum will be influenced or controlled by Cornwall organisations, but local (sub-Cornwall) organisations have to competitively bid against each other to win these resources. Meanwhile about 80% of the budget has just been plonked into the budgets of national agencies and cannot be influenced locally.

At sub-regional level, agglomeration of economic development functions into a coordinated and managed approach has, in large part, not yet happened. With a plethora of delivery organisations and a variety of strategic planning processes interwoven by organisations working on different geographies, it is extremely difficult to deliver economic and social objectives in a coordinated and, more importantly, effective manner. In Cornwall we have the advantage of clear geographical boundaries without economic leakage of the actions we take, but until quite recently very little control or influence over the economic development agenda. In order to gain some influence we have produced an overarching economic strategy.

This has, over a ten-year period, been successful in both coordinating a vision and focus for Cornwall's economy and getting 'buy in' from the private, community and public sector on what is needed for the county. However, there is still insufficient local influence over the actual delivery of the strategy, much of which is in the control of national or regional agencies, too often determined by their own national or regional agendas, some of which are just not right for the county. In order to make sure that both strategy and delivery are better controlled/influenced by Cornwall, we are proposing to establish a Cornwall Development Agency under the aegis of the new Cornwall Unitary Authority and with national, regional and European resources and services under its control.

This proposal is not stimulated by the cry, of which some may be aware, for Cornwall as an independent region or nation, but by a need to join up policy and delivery at a local level. This is why the Sub-National Review of Economic Development is so important not only in creating a new strategic approach but also in providing a solution to the delivery coordination problem. It is vital that strategic and delivery organisations of this type are established as widely as possible throughout the country, backed by local authorities and their partners and by government encouragement within the framework of a new settlement that determines responsibilities at national, regional and local levels.

Second, the current obsession in all areas of the public sector to ensure a split between strategy and delivery also provides for some distortions in effectiveness. There is a different mindset and approach between strategy and delivery, but they must be interlinked to be effective. Ensuring that there is a separation between the two can create an artificial chasm. It often seems that the split is much more about where you are in the geographical or political pecking order rather than to do with improving the effectiveness of public policy.

Is, for instance, all UK economic policy deemed to be strategic and national and therefore any actions in that policy area done on a non-national basis, just delivery? Similarly, is the regional level strategic and sub-regional merely delivery? How far does this extend? Have Parish Councils no role in policy development, only in delivery? This pecking order approach resulting from the split between strategy and delivery, has a number of effects: (1) it makes the strategic level feel important and in charge; (2) it can result in the strategic level disassociating itself from any responsibility for the delivery of its strategy; (3) the strategy can be ill-informed relying too much on evidence of statistics rather than the evidence and knowledge of practitioners; (4) it can result in an obsession by delivery partners with the delivery of targets rather than outcomes; (5) if the deliverer has no ownership of the rationale for its work, organisations and staff become cynical about their contribution, are not innovative and the feedback loop to policy is lost; and (6) too often it assumes that strategy and thinking is the difficult bit and delivery is the easy task, whereas experience would suggest the opposite.

Particularly in economic development work, strategy and delivery are mixed on a daily basis and it is sometimes difficult to make the distinction. Ensuring that strategy and delivery feed off each other rather than artificially creating separations is important in ensuring effectiveness in economic development work.

Third, it is vital that economic development at a local level ensures outcomes for the customers it is intended to serve whether those customers are businesses, people or communities. In the rush to develop strategies or the structure of organisations, and determining who is in charge, the customer is too often forgotten. It is vital that the cultural ethos of sub-regional economic development organisations is fit for purpose. Because economic development and regeneration activity draws from a broad church of skills and professions, existing organisations rarely have similar cultures. Regeneration and economic development organisations deal with multidimensional problems and therefore need a wide skill set to provide a multidimensional solution to these problems.

Different skill sets, as well as leaders with different backgrounds, produce different cultures. Too often organisations start with an immense burst of excitement, sometimes followed by success, and then, if not managed, a gradual decline in purpose and vision. It is the internal culture of organisations that provides, subject of course to external political or strategic about-turns, the long-term viability of delivery and transformation of local economies and communities.

So what is the right organisational culture for economic development organisations? What framework of people management provides the best results for regeneration and development organisation? The answer is not simple, as the work and circumstances vary substantially, but there are perhaps some principles that could be adopted.

The excellent sub-regional economic development or regeneration organisation should be clearly customer focused. This should be easier to achieve compared to national or regional actions given the small geography of subregions. Furthermore they must be able to show the effect of their actions at not only a superficial level of customers assisted but at a deeper economic or community level. How many actions taken in the name of economic regeneration can professionals, hand on heart, confirm have had an impact on GDP or community cohesion. In Cornwall it is planned to undertake some work in this area to identify which actions create the most benefit to the area; for example, is it a new airport or the amount of business advice that makes the difference?

Organisations also need to be entrepreneurial and innovative. Without new approaches to economic development, new projects and change or transformational leadership, local areas may or may not improve their economies, but there will not be a step change in their fortunes. However, if there is an overemphasis on innovation caused by constant 'initiative-itis' there is a danger of loss of purpose and vision for the area. There is also a need for systems and performance control, but it must be of the right type, and in particular be focussed on strong financial management, rather than chasing the output figures or following government targets too rigidly. Indeed there is an argument that any set target can be easily met in an economic development or regeneration organisation, because they are not really hard outputs. However, if the finances go wrong, there is all hell to pay.

One of the privileges of working in economic development and regeneration is that, compared to other public sector delivery such as in the health service, the outputs required are not only difficult to pin down but also difficult to measure. This allows the individual professional greater freedom to shape a service for local needs and demands. However, this privilege must come with a sense of responsibility to ensure that the organisation's and the individual's work is effective. Each year an individual and organisation should assess itself to ensure that it has made a difference, and is not claiming other's successes, too often a fault-line in the profession.

The background of the leadership of the organisation is also critical to the emphasis of its work. There are some chief executives who can only relate to economic development through physical development schemes and who prefer to employ surveyors close to them, others who are deal makers, others who run the organisation like a business, others whose focus is driven by business success, others who believe in influence and partnership, some focus on the policy requirements handed to them from above, some focus on the benefits that regeneration brings to the residents of the area and others, in a postmodern methodology, believe that as long as their name is in the newspapers and they appear on broadcast media, they will be successful. None of these leadership approaches are wrong, but none of them are entirely satisfactory. It is essential that the leadership of economic development and regeneration organisations embraces as broad a range of these characteristics as possible.

Overall, the key criteria for the culture of economic development organisation are as follows:

- a strong sense of purpose, public sector ethos and ownership of the issues
- a customer-focused business efficiency culture
- innovative and entrepreneurial climate without slipping into permanent revolution
- communication systems as strong internally as they are externally with transparency for all stakeholders
- strong financial systems.

Critical to the next few years of local economic development and regeneration is the successful implementation of the Sub-National Review in all regions. This requires the local authority to take the lead, and Whitehall departments and the RDA to let go a little more power. It does require a new settlement between central and strategic local government, a clear vision for the local area signed up to by all partners, and the creation of an organisational capacity derived from a consolidation of existing activities to a new set-up led by the local authority. The linkage between strategy and delivery must be maintained to ensure that the ultimate customer gets good quality service. Lastly, it is the culture of these new economic development organisations that will form the bedrock of the type of success and failure for the area they serve.

IN PERSPECTIVE

Building an Economic Development and Regeneration Future for Lincolnshire County Council

IVAN ANNIBAL[1]

Lincolnshire is almost as large as Northern Ireland with a population roughly the size of Sheffield. It has one County Council, seven second-tier authorities and over 500 town and parish councils. This makes its governance complex.

The County is a virtual island, bounded at the north by the Humber, at the east by the North Sea, at the south by the Fens and at the west by the Trent. Notwithstanding this relative inaccessibility it is effectively defined by the pull of settlements outside its boundaries. Humberside in the north, Peterborough in the south and Nottingham in the west.[2]

I have always seen the County as comprising five subeconomies:

- the A1 corridor – centred on Grantham
- Greater Lincoln – which accounts for 40% of the economy of the whole county

[1] I am Managing Director of Globe Regeneration Ltd and Assistant Director for Development (job share) at Lincolnshire County Council. These are my own independent views.

[2] For a very clear and encyclopaedic exposition of the economic geography of Lincolnshire see the Lincolnshire Research Observatory: www.research-lincs.org.uk

- the Food Hub – a billion pound per annum cluster of food processing and distribution centred on Spalding and Boston
- the seaside coast – a peripheral resort-based economy spanning Skegness and Mablethorpe
- The Lincolnshire heartlands – a network of market towns in a line travelling west to east from Gainsborough to Louth and south through Sleaford towards the Fens.

Despite the large and complex nature of our economy, Lincolnshire does have a sense of identity and incipient common purpose. Ironically it is those at the fringes of the County who have the strongest sense of a Lincolnshire identity. Sometimes this extends beyond our administrative boundaries. It is no surprise to me that, post-Humberside, the two new unitaries on the south bank of the Humber, chose to call themselves North and North East Lincolnshire rather than South and South East Humberside.

I deliberately used the term 'incipient common purpose' earlier because whilst there is no doubt that if you scratch a Lincolnshire local authority it will 'bleed Lincolnshire', I think we can do more to develop a sense of clear shared priorities.

Turning to our history of doing regeneration, Lincolnshire has sometimes become snarled up in debates about governance and process issues because of its complex geography and crowded institutional stage. In spite of this we have still delivered a significant number of transformational projects around economic development including: a £12 million broadband programme; a £5 million investment in the Spalding food-cluster with the University of Lincoln at Holbeach and a waterways regeneration strategy worth over £10 million. The level of ambition at the County Council, in this regard, is reflected in their decision in 2000 to borrow £50 million to provide a genuine additional match-funding pot to ensure we maximised the drawdown of Objective 2 funding into Lincolnshire.

Recently I have noticed that we are getting better at drawing things together around more of a common purpose and focusing less on the negative aspects of process debates. I suspect this is driven by the optimistic mood music coming out of the Review of Sub-National Economic Development and Regeneration (HM Treasury, 2007).

Another key 'joining up' factor is our decision, in the recent discussions, stimulated by the Local Government White Paper (DCLG, 2006), to progress down the slightly murky but ultimately more inclusive pathfinder route towards the 'virtual unitary'. In those two tier areas where the 'unitary genie' has been fully let out of the bottle the potential for joint working has been, in some cases, seriously compromised.

Our pathfinder approach has stimulated a range of discussions about enhanced joint working. These discussions provide a very useful context for the consideration of the issues arising for Lincolnshire from the Sub-National Review.

The other context for the evolution of approaches to economic regeneration in Lincolnshire, is the experience, of sub-regional engagement with the RDA. Since 1999 Lincolnshire has been the recipient of a Sub-Regional Strategic Partnership,[3] established around an EMDA structural template, to oversee the distribution of their funding in Lincolnshire. Occasionally the structure and role of the SSP has made joined up working across the board in Lincolnshire tricky.

This has often been as a consequence of the challenging bidding and funding requirements linked to accessing resources through the SSP. In view of the small size of most Lincolnshire Districts and their consequent limited capacity around regeneration, working up bids to the SSP has involved significant demands in terms of staff time. It has also sometimes challenged a sense of common purpose through competition for funding.

Recently the development of Sub-Regional Investment Plans as a means of drawing down resources to the SSP level, which are widely owned, consulted on and focused, has worked more effectively.

Looking to the future, the focus of the Sub-National Review has given some real new opportunities to local government. The recognition that economies work on a sub-regional basis[4] allied with the policy imperative of 'place shaping' puts local authorities right at the heart of regeneration delivery. The challenge in responding to this is for local authorities to make good on the new opportunities which are being offered to them. This will be a bigger challenge than many appreciate and should not be taken lightly – sometimes it is important to be careful what you wish for!

I have no doubt that local authorities should be placed at the heart of regeneration. Our challenge in Lincolnshire, however, is to take the route map set out for economic regeneration in the SNR, the opportunities around the development of the virtual unitary in Lincolnshire arising from the pathfinder approach and the evolution of our relationship with EMDA, to develop new ways forward. These approaches need to be fit for purpose and work for all players from the regional tier downwards.

Previous models for 'doing business' around economic development, outside of local authorities, have emphasised the role of the private sector as a leader.

Whilst it is clear that the private sector has much to contribute it is the democratically elected representatives of communities who should be allowed to lead public sector involvement in the economic development agenda. I am very optimistic that the implementation of the Sub-National Review proposals will provide real opportunities, not only for local authorities to return to the heart of public policy in terms of economic development, but that elected members will be given enhanced opportunities to drive that agenda. These opportunities will be through,

---

[3] See www.lincse.org.uk

[4] In addition to the blurb in the SNR see also the excellent Local Government Association (2007).

for example, a rebalancing of the board membership of the SSPs in the East Midlands in general and Lincolnshire in particular.

Central to the future is the need to balance governance and process considerations alongside our tradition of project delivery. We need to ensure we not only get our ducks in a row in relation to these 'internal' issues, but that we concentrate our efforts on tackling the actual economic challenges faced by the County to maximise its potential.

The GVA of Lincolnshire is just over 75% of the national average (Lincolnshire Enterprise, 2006). The County has, notwithstanding this, real opportunity areas and has recently achieved 'Growth Point Status' for its two largest settlements; Grantham and Lincoln. Each of the five subeconomies described earlier have their unique development challenges and opportunities. I can see a vision for Lincolnshire, which notwithstanding its low GVA, is very bright.

We have considerable benefits, which can be realised in terms of economic outcomes relating to the quality of our landscapes.[5] We develop good learning outcomes but leech out our young talent. However, we do attract skilled workers with families. We have a workforce that in some stubborn areas is part of a low wage–low skill equilibrium. On the upside we also have a relatively new University, which has made a huge contribution to the development of our economic competitiveness.

We have undertaken some long and detailed thinking about how to progress in the light of all the issues I have set out. This has involved a good deal of shuttle diplomacy amongst local authorities, our SSP and the private and community sectors. As people in Lincolnshire often mean what they don't say in public, a good deal of our discourse has been in private and informal meetings. This has enabled us to build on a very positive characteristic about how things happen in Lincolnshire, when organisations do commit to something they invariably really stick to it. A new model is emerging. It is based on design principles that should enable us to pool resources and expertise to focus our activities and outcomes.

We have come up with a three-phase concept for economic regeneration. It is based on the approach of splitting: policy, commissioning (described in some quarters as procurement) and delivery. The policy setting process for the new model involves recognising that each category of stakeholders involved in regeneration in Lincolnshire will have, and has, the right to express, a unique policy agenda. Each stakeholder organisation will be encouraged to refresh and reconfirm their policy perspectives as part of the establishment of the new approach.

This then provides a starting point for the development of a commissioning process. Where we can identify common ground as the 'Lincolnshire collective' through this process of policy discussions we intend to create one jointly staffed commissioning body. This body will look at the individual policy and strategy documents of its participants and

[5] For an exposition of the undervalued economic importance of landscape, which predates 'place shaping', see Rushbrook and Winter (2003).

consider how to most effectively build synergies amongst them to establish a common delivery agenda.

The County Council, EMDA and other local authorities will be encouraged to identify as many of their resources as possible to deploy through this body. It will pool capacity in terms of economic development expertise to act as an 'intelligent client' for Lincolnshire. Its role on behalf of its investors will be to commission the delivery of economic outcomes.

There is scope to evolve the present SSP in Lincolnshire to perform this role, supplemented by additional staffing from local authorities and others and with refreshed governance arrangements that will enable it be more proportionately 'owned' by its stakeholders.

The final stage in the process is, then, to look at delivery. Where participating organisations wish to retain aspects of direct delivery themselves we would encourage them, through the refreshed LAA, which will be shaped to reflect our new overall approach, to relate their activities to the bigger picture work of the joint commissioning agenda.

We anticipate commissioning delivery from the following:

- local authorities potentially working cross boundary, mediated through the new pathfinder arrangements
- Lincolnshire-based place-shaping delivery vehicles such as: Investors in Lincoln and Boston Area Regeneration Company
- emerging Growth Point partnerships in Lincoln and Grantham
- a proposed coastal regeneration company
- the private sector
- the voluntary sector.

It is probably useful at this juncture to reflect on the broader issues concerning the role of the private sector. I have not drawn much attention to them up to now. This is not because they do not have a key role to play. Private sector organisations are involved in the leadership of key economic groups such as the SSP, they provide services directly to local authorities and other regeneration agencies in Lincolnshire and they are by far and away the biggest driving force in our economy.

We have to engage with the private sector carefully and considerately if we are to generate quality involvement from them. We need to offer them meaningful and stimulating opportunities to add value.

Before summarising my narrative I should perhaps say a little about the paraphernalia of Local Strategic Partnerships (LSPs) and Local Area Agreements (LAAs). A textbook approach to economic development would have put the structure of the LSP and the LAA at the heart of economic development in Lincolnshire or, come to think of it, any area in England. The reality is that it has taken a long time for the structures around LSPs (we have eight in Lincolnshire for a population of less than 700,000 people) and LAAs to get embedded. This means that they tend to act more as a mirror for activity than the means by which business is done. This is reflected in the seven district and one county Sustainable Community Strategies that are 'live' in Lincolnshire. From a central government perspective these structures, in 'two-tier land', are the only 'show in town' – albeit there is scope to join up single models of activity cross boundary now through MAAs – we therefore need to ensure we build engagement and meaning into and through them in future.

In summary, then – the challenge of building a future around economic regeneration in Lincolnshire is analogous to herding cats. It involves trying to squeeze a complex spatial and organisational geography, against the background of a new national enthusiasm for sub-regional economic development, into a logical way forward. Lincolnshire, however, has massive potential and there is therefore huge merit in the task.

At the heart of my favoured approach for Lincolnshire is the development of a new means of joining the work of economic development actors up through commissioning. This methodology respects the right of individual organisations to have their own policy perspectives. It offers them the capacity to share in the development of an 'intelligent client' role. It removes much of the opportunity cost of competing for resources through bidding. Finally, it refocuses our thinking about our capacity to deliver economic outcomes, in our own backyard, creating the potential to harness a range of sub-county delivery vehicles, developed on a 'best fit' basis in terms of local circumstances and rooted in the new logic of place shaping.

One final thought – whilst getting the process right we need to keep our eye on the main challenge, which is delivery – 'it's the economy stupid!'[6]

References

DCLG (October 2006) *Strong and Prosperous Communities – The Local Government White Paper* (London: DCLG).

HM Treasury (July 2007) *Sub-National Review of Economic Development and Regeneration* (London: HM Treasury).

Lincolnshire Enterprise (2006) *Lincolnshire Economy Strategy*. Available at www.lincolnshire-enterprise.com.

Local Government Association (January 2007) *Prosperous Communities II*.

Other Key Documents

East Midlands Development Agency *A Flourishing Region: Regional Economic Strategy for the East Midlands 2006–2020*.

Lincolnshire Assembly (County Tier LSP) (2006) *Lincolnshire Sustainable Community Strategy*.

Lincolnshire County Council (2007) *Economic Development Strategy*.

Rushbrook & Winter (May 2003) *Literature Review of the Rural Economy* (Defra).

---

[6] The phrase, coined by Clinton campaign strategist James Carville, refers to the notion that Clinton was a better choice because Bush had not adequately addressed the economy, which was undergoing a recession at the time (Wikipedia, 2007).

A Personal View on How the Role of the RDA Regeneration Practitioner will Change as a Result of SNR

TOM WARBURTON

The implementation of the Sub-national Review (SNR) will radically change the skill sets needed at different 'levels' in the business of economic development, regeneration policy and delivery in the public sector. The resulting challenges for regional development agencies (RDAs), charged with leading the development of the first Integrated Regional Strategies, are many – not least in adapting to their new spatial responsibilities and an increased commissioning role.

If the SNR is to result in better outcomes, the right capacity and capability must be in the right place, at the right time. The RDA regeneration practitioner will require a wider range of spatial and planning skills; improved capacity to commission and manage complex projects rather than development and delivery skills; and ever-greater strategic vision.

In considering the skills challenges facing RDAs and the lessons they will have to learn during this transition phase, a reminder of their existing approach to place shaping and economic development is, first, relevant.

In our rapidly developing knowledge-based economy, an increasingly important driver of economic performance is quality of place. The 'offer' of our cities and towns is an essential part of attracting and retaining world-class businesses, entrepreneurs and highly skilled workers. For RDAs, this means that:

- we need to raise the quality of our places to match or exceed the quality of comparable places around the world, and to do this in such a way that they are sustainable in a more resource-poor, carbon-rationed world
- improving quality of place goes hand in hand with other interventions to raise the economic performance of our regions, such as business support, skills development and economic inclusion – integration is key.

Place shaping is, however, complex. Different issues must be tackled at the national, regional, sub-regional and local levels; the joining up of many policy areas such as housing, transport, planning and environmental performance is a necessity, yet this coordination and integration requires high levels of technical, managerial and leadership skills.

The use of intelligent data analysis is vital to establish the links between issues such as housing and economic growth and, subsequently, how spatial planning at the regional and sub-regional level can be used to support growth in the right places. Tools such as Multi Area Agreements are central to strategic planning at this level.

Investment from and engagement with the private sector is a key part of the mechanism, to support the physical and strategic infrastructure needed, facilitate the brokerage of deals and to establish partnerships for development and regeneration. And, of course, the continuing challenge of balancing growth and managing decline is in sharper focus than ever before, given the serious resource and climate change issues we face.

RDAs, together with our partners, have developed an understanding of the distinctive role and contribution of different places to regional economic performance, with the aim of focusing public and private sector investment to match this. For example, cities are key to accelerating economic growth but, within cities, there is also extreme disadvantage. Enabling cities to fulfil their potential requires a strategy tailored to each locality, set in context of a regional strategy. This must be supported by:

- coordinated public policy and investment
- strong leadership
- appropriate capacity and capability at the right level, and
- clear governance.

Similar principles can be applied to the increasingly diverse nature of the rural economy, with some knowledge-based businesses choosing to locate in rural areas where they can use digital technology to reach markets beyond their immediate locality.

The twin ambitions of Sir Michael Lyons' Review of Local Government – for local authorities to be place-shapers and for the Department for Communities and Local Government to create sustainable, prosperous communities – require effective regional arrangements that are capable of adding real value, providing the strategic context and expertise in delivery that will enable national objectives to be met in locally determined ways.

However, the SNR outlined the way in which current regional governance has become somewhat cluttered, with an unduly complex regional strategy framework and a structure lacking in clarity of purpose, with the consequent risk of duplication and inefficiency.

The resulting recommendations demand skills development and consolidation of existing capability right across the board, if we are to meet the challenge of developing the first integrated regional strategies effectively. For RDAs, at regional level, this means further strengthening our existing partnership working, and recognising that agencies will be working in a far more political context.

First, local authorities will be key strategic and delivery partners in the implementation of SNR. They are at the very centre of creating great places to live, work and visit; fundamental to place shaping both in terms of process and planning and of local vision, influence and community engagement. Sustainable communities depend on their collective leadership, strong vision and strategy at local level.

In several regions of England, that transition period will also coincide with huge changes in local government structure. In North East England alone, Northumberland and County Durham will become unitary authorities. Whilst we welcome the clear leadership, strategic focus and improved capacity to support economic development and regeneration that this will provide and look forward to building on our already close working relationships, there can be no doubt that we will be expecting a great deal from the new authorities in their fledgling years.

The SNR proposes more delegation to sub-regional level, but are the skills and capacity there? Robust transition arrangements will lay the ground and RDAs are already working very closely with Government to develop proposals for this. SNR sets out an increase in regional influence over national spending on priorities such as transport, housing and skills, and calls for the work of national agencies to complement regional priorities. RDAs will need to exercise ever more effective leadership and engagement skills in working with politicians and political processes, both at local and national level.

Our capacity for evidence gathering and analysis is another key area for development. We are clear about the central role of a good quality evidence base, in living up to the challenges posed by the SNR. We are equally clear that we need to work harder to get this right. Success in delivering an influential evidence base will depend to a large extent on both the analytical capacity within regions and, crucially, the way we work together as partners.

Building better links between the academic community and regional policy makers, plus effective investment in the skills of the regional analytical community, are key. But it is an open and inclusive approach to framing and delivering our evidence base that will underpin successful development of Integrated Regional Strategies. A shared research agenda and evidence base will help us work through some of the tough choices that we will all need to make in shaping regional policy and funding priorities.

The stronger role for RDAs as commissioners rather than direct delivery bodies is perhaps one of the main areas of skills shift for the agencies. The contracting of complex, multidisciplinary programmes will demand a very specific skill set, along with increased capacity for monitoring and evaluation.

Finally, the RDAs must continue to develop their close engagement with the private sector. The agencies are business-led, and the participation of private sector business in the development of regional economic and spatial strategy is already at the core of our successful policy making and delivery. Private sector investment and engagement will continue to be crucial in ensuring we have the capacity and capability we will need to deliver the recommendations of the SNR, and in helping to tackle some of the difficult issues raised by the concept of an Integrated Regional Strategy. The current business-led board structure of RDAs is working well, and the agencies strongly believe that this should continue as a tool to drive that task.

But, as well as addressing skills needs, the SNR transition will also be a learning phase for RDAs. Agencies will have to delegate more responsibility. For some, there is the need to increase strategic thinking and the development of a long-term view. As already discussed, agencies will be working within a much more political context, under more robust scrutiny and governance arrangements. They will be called upon to exercise strong, strategic, decision making.

The SNR is a chance to move towards a more sophisticated policy approach that could have huge benefits for English regions. However, the size of the task ahead cannot be underestimated if this transition is to be made effectively. The review sets out a very ambitious agenda, which means change and more effective integration across all levels of involvement in regeneration. RDAs fully recognise that their capacity and capability will need to be substantial, given the technical and political challenges it presents.

Thus, as agencies set out on this transition, I suggest that they have a dual role to play – in both developing the new Integrated Regional Strategy and in building the capacity of our partners to deliver effective regeneration, using our economic expertise and track record of private sector engagement.

Index

Page numbers in *Italics* represent tables.
Page numbers in **Bold** represent figures.